Insights from Performance Criticism

Insights from Performance Criticism

Peter S. Perry

Fortress Press
Minneapolis

INSIGHTS FROM PERFORMANCE CRITICISM

Cover image: Brooklyn Bridge/Andres Garcia Martin/Thinkstock & Cruz de Tejeda/emregologlu/Thinkstock

Cover design: Laurie Ingram

Library of Congress Cataloging-in-Publication Data
Print ISBN: 978-1-5064-0016-7
eBook ISBN: 978-1-5064-0112-6

The paper used in this publication meets the minimum requirements of American National Standard for Information Sciences — Permanence of Paper for Printed Library Materials, ANSI Z329.48-1984.
Manufactured in the U.S.A.

This book was produced using Pressbooks.com, and PDF rendering was done by PrinceXML.

Contents

Series Foreword

"What does this mean?"

That is, perhaps, the most-asked question with regard to the Bible. What does this verse mean? What does this story mean? What does this psalm or letter or prophecy or promise or commandment mean?

The question can arise from a simple desire for information, or the concern may be one of context or relevance: What *did* this mean to its original audience? What *does* it mean for us today?

Someone has said that understanding the Bible is difficult not because meaning is hard to find but because it is so abundant. The problem for interpreters is not *too little meaning* but *too much.* The question becomes, which of all the possible meanings is to be preferred?

But is that really a problem? And, if so, is it not a lovely one?

This abundance of meaning became especially clear in the last decades of the twentieth century when the field of biblical studies embraced dozens of new methods and approaches that had not previously been used or appreciated within the guild. In many ways, biblical studies became more exciting than ever before.

But, yes, the task of understanding the Bible could be daunting. Bible teachers, clergy and lay, who had struggled through college or seminary to learn "the historical-critical method" were suddenly confronted with novel strategies drawn from many other fields of inquiry: sociology, psychology, world religions, cultural anthropology, communication theory, modern literary criticism, and so forth. Then came the avalanche of interpretive approaches grounded in particular philosophical or ideological perspectives: feminism, postmodernism, liberation theology, postcolonialism, queer theology, and on and on.

For the open minded, the yield was an embarrassment of riches. We now understand the Bible in so many different ways: its historical witness, its theological message, its emotional impact, its sociocultural significance, its literary artistry, its capacity for rhetorical engagement, and so on.

At this point in time, we probably understand the Bible better than any who have gone before us. The Bible may challenge us more deeply than it challenged our forebears—and, yet, we have discovered that the Bible also seems to invite us (perhaps to *dare* us) to challenge it back. Many insights into the meaning of Scripture have come from people doing exactly that.

This *Insights* series from Fortress Press presents brief volumes that describe the different ways in which modern scholars approach the Bible, with emphasis on what we have learned from each of these approaches. These are not boring books on esoteric methodology. Some attention, of course, needs to be paid to presumptions and procedures, but the emphasis in each book is on the practical "pay-off" that a given approach has for students and teachers of the Bible. The authors discuss the most important insights they have gained from their approaches and they provide examples of how those insights play out when working with specific biblical texts in actual real-world circumstances.

Each volume discusses:

- how a particular method, approach, or strategy was first developed and how its application has changed over time;
- what current questions arise from its use;
- what enduring insights it has produced; and
- what questions remain for future scholarship.

Some volumes feature traditional approaches while others focus on new and experimental ones. You will definitely learn things in every book. Your current understanding of "what the Bible means" will be increased. And if you find that the "type of meaning" gained from a particular approach is not what interests you, perhaps you will nevertheless be grateful for the brief tour of a topic that fascinates some of your peers. The books are intentionally brief: they allow us to sample strategies and perspectives, to look down various avenues and see where they lead. They facilitate informed decisions regarding where we might want to go next.

I trust that we are now past the point of arguing over which approach to Scripture is the correct one. Such squabbles were part of the growth pains associated with the guild's aforementioned discovery that meaning is abundant, not so much elusive as ubiquitous.

Those of us who were professors during the late twentieth century sometimes helped our students deal with the methodological confusion by reminding them of the old Indian fable about six blind men and an elephant. In one well-known version of that tale, each of the blind men encounters an elephant and decides "what an elephant is like" based on his singular experience: one feels the trunk and says an elephant is like a hose; another, the tusk and says it is like a spear; another, the ear and says it is like a fan; another, the side and says it is like a wall; another, the leg and says it is like a tree; another, the tail and says it is like a rope. Later, when the men compare notes, each of them insists that he alone understands what an elephant is like: his comrades are totally mistaken.

So, we told our students in the 1990s, each biblical approach or method yields some valid insight into "the meaning of the Bible" (or into "the mystery of divine revelation" or into "what God wants to say to us"). But we would be wise to listen to those whose experience with the Bible is different from ours.

The Insights series is born of humility: its very existence is testimony to our commitment that we need to compare notes about the Bible with openness to each other's diverse perspectives. But, beyond that, I would hope that these volumes might also lead us to admit the limits of our perception. We now see, as the apostle Paul puts it, "in a mirror dimly" (1 Cor 13:12)

Many, including myself, who study the Bible believe it is the word of God, meaning it is a source of divine revelation. For this reason alone, the meaning of the Bible is abundant and ubiquitous.

We probably understand the Bible here and now better than any other people in history, and this triumph has brought us to the realization of how little we can understand, now or ever. But, insights? Yes. Those we can claim. Our experiences, our knowledge, and our perspectives do have authenticity and from them we have at least gained some *insights* into the meaning of Scripture. Time to compare notes!

MARK ALLAN POWELL

Preface

This book is a synthesis of my experiences with many far wiser and more knowledgeable people who have studied and developed performance criticism. I have tried to acknowledge my debt to them in the footnotes, so please read those! I am especially indebted to my mentor, David Rhoads, who coined the term "biblical performance criticism," and James Maxey, my colleague from the beginning of our doctoral studies with Dr. Rhoads. I am grateful for our conversations over the last twelve years. Both of these kind souls read an early draft of chapter 1 of this book and gave significant feedback. I am also grateful to Jeanette Mathews who inspired me to use Habakkuk as an example and gave her feedback on chapter 3. From the endnotes and bibliography, I have surely left out significant people who have contributed to this emerging discipline. Many more references and information can be found at the website www.BiblicalPerformanceCriticism.org. I pray, forgiving reader, that you will discover these unattributed treasures through further reading, study, and conversation.

This book also synthesizes my experiences as a performer and the many audiences that have given me feedback. I am grateful to audiences in Arizona and Illinois that have opened up their classrooms and congregations for me to perform. They are a part of this book, too.

Inevitably, this is my synthesis and no one else's. I cannot claim that it represents a consensus picture of performance criticism. Some scholars doing work related to performance criticism will disagree with details and methods. I have made performance studies important, especially the work of the late Dwight Conquergood, in a way that only a few other performance critics have done. Second, I use relevance theory as the basic theory of human communication. Others do not explicitly describe their theory of human communication, while others would choose a different theory of how signs work (called "semiotics," e.g., by the nineteenth-century philosopher Charles S. Peirce; I don't think the different theories are incompatible). Third, I believe that scholars should perform texts with audiences in order to truly understand them.

This synthesis also inevitably reflects my social situation. I am a Lutheran Christian pastor in the United States writing in English from a relatively privileged position. As I will say in the conclusion, those who practice performance criticism need to be challenged for the ways we may try to universalize insights and lose sight of the particular cultural situation. At its best, I think performance criticism offers a method and practice for becoming more sensitive to the social locations of the performer and audience.

Thanks to Susan Hannah for her proofreading of the manuscript and valuable comments. I find it difficult to adequately express my gratitude for my wife, Dana, and daughters, Ruth and Esther, whose support, patience, and grace is a daily gift from God.

My goal is to persuade the reader that biblical performance criticism offers insights that make it worth your time to try out for yourself. It has changed my life, my scholarship, and my ministry.

Soli Deo gloria!

1

The Performed Text

Introduction

Biblical Performance Criticism is a way of understanding the Bible. It is the result of many streams of thought meeting over the last century, including form criticism, oral-tradition studies, rhetorical criticism, narrative criticism, memory studies, media studies, and performance studies. In some way, each of these streams analyzes four elements: (1) someone speaking, (2) someone hearing, (3) a text, and (4) a social situation. Each has contributed to the understanding that the Bible should be read in terms of the interaction of those four elements rather than any one of them in isolation.

- *Form criticism*, developed at the end of the nineteenth century, is based on the fact that biblical authors drew on oral traditions to compose their writings. Form critics try to classify a passage by its genre or form (e.g., parables, pithy sayings, conflict stories) and to find the social situation in which that form might have been used.[1]

1. Hermann Gunkel (1862–1932) is usually credited for conceiving form criticism, which was further developed by Martin Noth, Gerhard von Rad, and Claus Westermann for the Hebrew Bible, and by Karl Ludwig Schmidt, Martin Dibelius, and Rudolf Bultmann for the New Testament. For a

- *Oral-tradition studies* emerged in the 1930s from the discovery that Bosnian folk storytellers used repeated scene types and formulas in a way that reminded scholars of Homer's Greek epic stories, the *Iliad* and *Odyssey*. With these set scene types and formulas, a storyteller could easily remember a story and adapt it for each new audience. It was natural that biblical scholars started to look for similar techniques in the Bible.[2]
- *Rhetoric* is the art of persuasion. Rhetorical critics analyze the way biblical authors try to persuade an audience. We know from ancient training books for speakers that they were taught to persuade not only with reason, but also with emotion. Speakers used the influence of personal characteristics, such as their virtue or standing in the community. Some speakers during biblical times used the sound of words to delight an audience, for example, by beginning a phrase with words that all begin with the same sound. Gestures, movement, and facial expressions were important to clarify and emphasize what was said.[3] Telling stories is one of the most common ways the Bible is shared.
- *Narrative criticism* provides indispensable tools to analyze how

helpful summary of scholarship up to 1986 with a focus on form criticism, see Robert C. Culley, "Oral Tradition and Biblical Studies," *Oral Tradition* 1, no. 1 (1986): 30-65. It can be accessed online at http://journal.oraltradition.org/files/articles/1i/3_culley.pdf. The articles at oraltradition.org are a treasure trove worth exploring.

2. Milman Parry developed the "oral-formulaic" theory that his student, Albert B. Lord, elaborated on in *The Singer of Tales* (Cambridge: Harvard University Press, 1960), and which Walter Ong and John Miles Foley further developed. Werner Kelber brought it into biblical studies in *The Oral and Written Gospel: The Hermeneutics of Speaking and Writing in the Synoptic Tradition, Mark, Paul, and Q* (Philadelphia: Fortress Press, 1983), as did Susan Niditch in her *Oral World and Written Word* (Louisville: Westminster John Knox, 1996). See also Raymond F. Person, "The Role of Memory in the Tradition Represented by the Deuteronomic History and the Book of Chronicles," *Oral Tradition* 26, no. 2 (October 2011): 537–50, http://journal.oraltradition.org/issues/26ii/person.
3. What I am describing is sometimes called "historic rhetorical criticism," perhaps first used by Hans Dieter Betz in *Galatians: A Commentary on Paul's Letter to the Churches in Galatia*, Hermeneia (Minneapolis: Fortress Press, 1989). Whitney Shiner used rhetorical handbooks in preparing his own performance of Mark; see his *Proclaiming the Gospel: First-Century Performance of Mark* (Harrisburg, PA: Trinity Press International, 2003). William David Shiell studied the persuasive use of gestures based on rhetorical handbooks in *Reading Acts: The Lector and the Early Christian Audience* (Leiden: Brill, 2004). Kathy Maxwell has studied how ancient rhetoricians anticipated audience interaction in *Hearing Between the Lines: The Audience as Fellow-Worker in Luke-Acts and Its Literary Milieu* (London: T&T Clark, 2010).

biblical texts are stories with characters, setting, time, plot, point of view, and standards of judgment.[4]

- *Memory studies* examine how memory is a social reality, shaped by how groups of people organize space and time and communicate these memories inside and outside the group. People collectively build and maintain memories by sharing what happened, correcting and elaborating the telling, and then retelling the memories. Some write a memory down, often as a way to remember it in a particular way or to share it to distant groups. These written memories often reflect techniques used to help remember complex material.[5]
- *Media studies* analyzes the way the medium of communication affects communication. Especially as television became more popular in the last half of the twentieth century, people became more aware of how the medium shaped the way both speakers spoke and hearers heard. Speakers were seen! Today, we have not only print media, but live radio, recorded audio, recorded video, live streaming video, and hyperlinked Internet resources. Few would go as far as Marshall McLuhan to say "the medium *is* the message," but scholars of media studies have helped us understand the possibilities and limitations of different media. Anyone who has seen a movie of a Bible story knows that the media of film is different than an experience of the printed page.[6]
- *Performance studies* emerged out of theater studies and cultural

4. See David Rhoads, Joanna Dewey, and Donald Mitchie, *Mark as Story: An Introduction to the Narrative of a Gospel*, 3d ed. (Minneapolis: Fortress Press, 2012); Mark Allan Powell, *What Is Narrative Criticism?*, Guides to Biblical Scholarship (Minneapolis: Fortress Press, 1991); and James L. Resseguie, *Narrative Criticism of the New Testament: An Introduction* (Grand Rapids: Baker, 2005).
5. Maurice Halbwachs initiated the modern study of social memory in 1925, followed by Jan Assman (who uses the term "cultural memory"). Birger Gerhardsson introduced memory as a category for understanding the transmission of the Gospels in 1961 with *Memory and Manuscript* (repub.: Grand Rapids: Eerdmans, 1998). See Tom Thatcher, *Why John Wrote a Gospel: Jesus—Memory—History* (Louisville: Westminster John Knox, 2005), and the collection edited by Alan Kirk and Tom Thatcher, *Memory, Tradition, and Text: Uses of the Past in Early Christianity* (Atlanta: SBL Press, 2005).
6. In 1987, Tom Boomershine was one of the first to reflect on media in biblical interpretation. See his "Biblical Megatrends: Towards a Paradigm for the Interpretation of the Bible in Electronic Media," in *SBL Seminar Papers* (Atlanta: Scholars Press, 1987), 144–57. John Miles Foley's Pathways Project is an exploration of the similarities and differences between Internet media and oral tradition. See www.pathwaysproject.org, and his book *Oral Tradition and the Internet: Pathways of the Mind* (Champaign: University of Illinois Press, 2012).

> anthropology to analyze any embodied action that is rehearsed and performed. "All the world's a stage," Shakespeare said. Performance studies looks everywhere for performances: in the home, in the classroom, in the marketplace, in religious gatherings, and everywhere people repeat behaviors for a group.[7]

Form criticism, oral-tradition studies, rhetorical criticism, narrative criticism, memory studies, media studies, and performance studies are seven ways of interpreting the Bible that contribute to what we are calling "biblical performance criticism." But all this sounds very abstract.

The concrete experience of performing a biblical passage has had an impact on me and others who have prepared, internalized, and performed for audiences. When scholars, pastors, teachers, and students have gone beyond the silent and individual interaction with the Bible, it has changed their way of thinking about it and the tasks of studying and teaching it. David Rhoads, Tom Boomershine, Margaret Lee, Whitney Shiner, Pam Faro, and James Maxey, to name a few, will never read the Bible in the same way again because they have performed biblical material. I began memorizing and performing Bible passages as a pastor. During my study of the book of Revelation, I translated and memorized it for performance. I have now performed it over a dozen times to different audiences, and each concrete performance event has given me new insights. *This book is an attempt to communicate the payoff for performing passages from the Bible and to persuade the reader to give it a try.*

The Bible is very concrete. It tells specific stories about people's experiences with God and is itself a response to encounters with God. It portrays named and unnamed people responding to one another in specific situations. It is used today in encounters with God in devotion,

7. Richard Schnechner (theater studies), Ervin Goffman (sociology), and Victor Turner (cultural anthropology) are often thought of as the parents of performance studies. See Richard Schechner, *Performance Studies: An Introduction*, 3d ed. (London: Routledge, 2013). For two examples of the impact on performance studies in biblical studies, see William Doan and Terry Giles, *Prophets, Performance, and Power* (London: Continuum, 2005), and Jeanette Mathews, *Performing Habakkuk: Faithful Re-Enactment in the Midst of Crisis* (Eugene, OR: Wipf & Stock, 2012).

prayer, and worship. People use it to comfort and to persuade others in concrete situations.

Therefore, to be concrete and get at the breadth of what we mean by "performance," consider twelve brief scenes, each based on a passage from the Bible or from early Christian writings. In each scene there are four elements: at least one performer, an audience, some reference to a "text," and a larger situation. These scenes are necessarily brief and not the detailed descriptions that we will strive for later. For each, ask yourself: Who is the performer? Who is the audience? How do audience and performer interact? What is the "text" and what role does it play in the scene? What else do you need to know about the situation to make sense of the scene? With all of these questions in view, what is "performance"?

Scene 1: *A father and his son sit in the shade of a tree on a sunny afternoon. The father asks his son to recite the Ten Commandments just as his father had asked him long ago. At first, his son launches quickly into it, "You shall have no other gods . . ." and recites the First, then the Second, and the Third Commandment. But then he hesitates on the first word of the Fourth Commandment, struggling to remember. His father begins to give him a hint, but his son asks, "Why do we do this, Father?" His father sighs. He nods his head before responding, "We were Pharaoh's slaves in Egypt, but the Lord brought us out of Egypt. . . ."*[8] *After telling the story of the people coming out of Egypt, the father resumes jogging his son's memory.*

This scene imagines Deut 6:20–24 in practice at some unspecified location at some unknown time. One way to describe it would be to say that the son is the performer who is asked to recite the Ten Words (more commonly known today as the "Ten Commandments" found in

8. See Proverbs 3 and Tobit 4 for other examples of fathers teaching their sons. David Carr shows how education was enculturation into a way of being. This education enculturation happened primarily in the context of family, first with proverbs and other kinds of wisdom literature for making wise choices, but later to enculturate Torah obedience. The instruction was oral and memorized. Recitation developed memory. Written materials supported education, even if not always accessed directly. Although most likely applicable only to elites and their families, Deuteronomy sets the goal of Torah education in every Jewish home no matter what socioeconomic position, an ideal that was picked up during Hasmonean rule (164–163 BCE). See David M. Carr, *Writing on the Tablet of the Heart: Origins of Scripture and Literature* (New York: Oxford University Press, 2008).

Deut 5:6–21) for his father, the audience. But we could also say the father is the performer and the son the audience. The son triggers his father's performance by the question, "Why do we do this?" and the father responds. He accepts the reversal of roles and becomes the performer. He performs a traditional response, which we now may find in Deut 6:20–24, but we have to admit that there is nothing with writing on it anywhere in the scene. The son is expected to have the "text" in his memory, not on a piece of paper. The father does not have a script in front of him, but remembers a traditional response that he was taught. Can we still call Deuteronomy 5 and 6 the "text" of this scene even though both father and son learned them completely by memory without a written reference? Does a "text" need to be present or even exist for this to be considered a performance? There are many details left out of the scene that would shape the impact of the event. If this scene was between an Israelite father and son during a peaceful time, say, in Solomon's early rule, the son's question may simply reflect his boredom. If the scene took place during a time when there was pressure for Jews to follow Greek customs, the son's question may be laced with fear and the father's nod may express recognition of the danger of publically expressing their faith. Performance in this scene means the father is enculturating his son, that is, he is developing in his son the values, attitudes, and behaviors of a group of people.

Scene 2: *Solomon may have built the temple in Jerusalem, but David organized the supplies needed to build it and the musicians who would play the instruments and sing about the great things God has done. It is a family affair: for example, a priest-musician Heman's fourteen sons and three daughters are under his direction. There are a variety of players on cymbals, harps, and lyres, while others sing. The scene shifts to Heman directing his children and 271 trained singers. There are students repeating exercises with teachers, each ready to sing aloud a song of thanksgiving and telling of God's wondrous deeds: "For the Lord is good! God's steadfast love endures forever, and God's faithfulness to all generations!" Finally, this ensemble sings for those who have come to the temple. The gathered people follow their lead and respond, "For God is good, for God's steadfast love endures forever!"*[9]

Performance may be more recognizable in this scene based on 1 Chronicles 25: the performance of instrumental music with singing. As with the father and son in the first scene, Heman and his children are engaged in enculturation: through repetition and practice, he and his children develop the practices of leading others in song. It shapes their identity, their responses to situations, and their relationships to God and one another. The scene shifts from the father teaching his children to the larger group of musicians who are performing and an audience who responds by repeating the refrain. There are no written materials described in the scene. The "text" is only in their memory, although today we may find the refrain many times in the Bible. The musical tune to which they sang these words, however, existed only in their memory and is now lost to us.

Scene 3: *Isaiah worked for years as a royal prophet, advising the king with messages from God, the King of the Universe. In 711 BCE, he heard that the Assyrian Empire (ruled by King Sargon II) conquered the city of Ashdod, on the Mediterranean coast, due west of Jerusalem. How will he get the king's attention that an alliance with Egypt and Ethiopia will not protect Judah from the Assyrians? Desperate times call for desperate measures: the royal prophet takes off all his clothes and goes naked and barefoot "with buttocks uncovered" for three years! To everyone who asks why, he proclaims, "God says the Egyptians and Ethiopians will be carried away naked and barefoot by the Assyrians. If this is what happened to those to whom we fled for help from Assyria, how shall we escape?" Sometimes words aren't enough to get people's attention.*

There is no exchange of roles in this scene from Isaiah 20: Isaiah is clearly the performer and the audience is the king and all who see his nakedness and inquire. As in the first two scenes, there is a give and take between performer and audience. Isaiah's body is central: he uses it to get attention, make an emotional impact, communicate without words, and illustrate his point. This exchange is written in what we now call "Isaiah chapter 20," but the scene describes no written

9. Quoting Ps 100:5; see also Ps 26:6–7. For situations using this kind of refrain, see 2 Chr 5:13 and 7:3, and Psalm 118.

materials.[10] What was his audience's response? Were they transformed by his performance? The book of Isaiah doesn't say. This is not Isaiah's only prophecy, but one in which his body played a critical role. How was his body a part of his other prophetic performances but not described in the text?

Scene 4: *Thousands of men and women gather early in the morning in the courtyard inside the fresh, new walls of Jerusalem. The priest Ezra climbs onto a newly constructed wooden platform with his back to the Water Gate, through which people haul water from the spring outside the gate. With six leaders on his right and seven on his left, he unrolls a large scroll: the Torah, the book of the Law of Moses, the instruction for God's people. The people stand up as they see him open the scroll. Before reading, he begins with a prayer, blessing the Lord as the great God and the people answer by saying, "Amen, Amen!" before bowing their faces to the ground in honor of God. Ezra and thirteen other leaders take turns reading from the Law and explaining it so that the people understand its meaning. Thirteen Levites, spread out through the crowd, further teach and explain to the people what it means. As the people begin to understand how they have not been living according to the Law, many break down in tears. But the governor, Nehemiah, won't let them wallow in guilt or fear but encourages gladness that God has given them the Law and that they understand it. They are sent to feast in joy and to share with those who have no food prepared.*[11]

Ezra and the other leaders perform the text of the Law of Moses for the assembled Judeans, a scene described in Neh 8:1–12. Some scholars question what really happened on that day and what really was read, but this is the way Nehemiah 8 tells the story. Ezra is not a solo performer; his is the most famous name to us, but he is reading the

10. Martti Nissinen writes, "the general conclusion may be drawn that ancient Near Eastern prophecy was basically oral performance, that is, delivery of verbal messages spoken by a prophet. The message could be transmitted orally by one or several go-betweens all the way through, from prophet to destination. Occasionally, but never quite systematically, the spoken word ended up in written form, for different purposes and under varying circumstances." Nissinen, "Spoken, Written, Quoted, and Invented: Orality and Writtenness in Ancient Near Eastern Prophecy," in *Writings and Speech in Israelite and Ancient Near Eastern Prophecy*, ed. Ehud Ben Zvi and Michael H. Floyd (Atlanta: SBL Press, 2000), 235–71, at 268.
11. See a similar story as Josiah's priests rediscover the Law in 2 Kgs 22:3–13.

text with other leaders. The reading is not continuous, but broken by pauses for explanation. Are the thirteen Levites also performers? They are helping the large crowd understand the reading, expanding and illustrating each passage perhaps with their own words and stories, as a jazz musician may riff on a musical theme. The crowd likely has questions to ask these explainers, a further give and take before the reading continues. There is ritual surrounding this reading. Before the reading, Ezra leads them in prayer and they respond with "Amen." Is this part of the performance? It shapes the situation: the prayer situates the reading in a relationship between the people and God, a relationship of gratitude for all God has done, and a relationship with the agreement of the people. ("Amen" means "yes" or "truly.") There is a written text: a scroll, and probably a very large one that may have required some help to hold and manage. In addition to the questions during the reading, some of the audience respond with tears, but Nehemiah the governor (not one of the original performers but whose presence adds significance and authority to the reading) assures them of reason for joy and encourages feasting and special attention to those who are without. A festive meal together is an important response by the audience to the performance, with consideration for those in need.

Scene 5: *A group has gathered in the public building of a small town in the hills of Galilee.*[12] *The village covers only a few acres; the group is composed largely of men who have time and influence to gather weekly for a reading from the Torah and the prophets and for teaching. The crowd is eager to hear from a man who grew up in the village. They have heard about his energetic and charismatic teaching in other places. After the Torah portion is read, this Jesus is called forward to read the portion from the prophets. He unrolls the scroll to the place in Isaiah and reads,*

"The Spirit of the Lord is upon me,

12. Lee I. Levine, "The Synagogues of Galilee," and David A. Fiensy, "The Galilean Village in the Late Second Temple and Mishnaic Periods," both in *Galilee in the Late Second Temple and Mishnaic Periods, Volume 1: Life, Culture, and Society*, ed. David A. Fiensy and James Riley Strange (Minneapolis: Fortress Press, 2014), 129–50, 177–207, respectively.

because he has anointed me
to bring good news to the poor.

He has sent me to proclaim release to the captives
and recovery of sight to the blind,
to let the oppressed go free,
to proclaim the year of the Lord's favor."

He rolls up the scroll, hands it back to the person who takes care of the scrolls, and then sits down to teach. The silence is pregnant as people wait for his words, and when he begins to teach he explains that this prophecy applies to him. Every detail applies to his task and purpose. He summarizes, "Today this scripture has been fulfilled in your hearing." The people respond to each other with amazement. Comments can be heard throughout the room. But a few begin to wonder aloud about this homegrown teacher, asking, "Isn't this Joseph's son?"

As with Ezra reading the Law, Jesus holds the scroll of Isaiah. Jesus stands to read and sits to interpret. Isaiah's original performance and situation is a faint echo behind the voice of this new situation. Isaiah proclaimed that he was the one proclaiming a year of freedom to those returning from exile in Babylon. Jesus makes the dramatic claim: this prophecy is about him and his situation! He is the one anointed by the Spirit. He is the one bringing good news. He is the one proclaiming release to the captives, sight to the blind, freedom for the oppressed. He is the one proclaiming the Lord's favor. Although the words are the same, the performer, the audience and the situation radically affect the meaning. At first the audience responds favorably, but quickly they wonder where this hometown boy comes off claiming so much. Audience responses can be diverse and even change during a performance!

As with the scene from Nehemiah 8, some scholars question the historical accuracy of the scene Luke describes (4:16–22), but such concerns are beside the point for our current purposes. Luke tells his story this way. When Luke 4 is read to an audience, it becomes a performance of Luke's portrayal of Jesus' performance, which includes performance of a passage from Isaiah 61. There are multiple performance events embedded within a performance of Luke 4 (a contemporary performance of Luke, Luke's performance of Jesus, Jesus' performance of Isaiah). What are the effects of this layered performance event for an audience in a specific situation?

Scene 6: *Jesus leads his disciples and a crowd up a mountainside, and begins to speak, "Blessed are the poor in spirit, for theirs is the kingdom of heaven. . . ." He goes on for about twenty-five minutes, referring to the Torah's instructions about murder, adultery, and divorce. He relates his teaching to ordinary things like salt, lamps, birds, and flowers. He talks about common ways to express faith in God, such as prayer, fasting, and giving to the poor. He speaks freely and passionately in a way that people remember.*

Matthew describes this scene, what we now call "the Sermon on the Mount" (Matthew 5–7), and his audience can easily imagine it: Jesus teaches an audience made up of disciples (people who have an ongoing relationship with him) and others who simply have heard of him and want to hear what he has to say. His teaching is unscripted, in the sense that he has nothing written down and everything committed to memory. Yet, his words seem hardly spontaneous but, rather, planned and composed in his mind. Each saying or story, such as the list of "Blessed are . . ." or comparing followers to salt and light, are building blocks that can be reused and reassembled with other blocks depending on the audience and situation. Matthew's audience can imagine Jesus said, "Blessed are the poor in spirit" on one occasion and simply "Blessed are the poor" on another, just like preachers who reuse and adapt stories and sayings because they find them effective.

Matthew writes, "Blessed are the poor in spirit" in his Gospel, while Luke writes simply, "Blessed are the poor." Perhaps they each have heard many versions and have produced composites. Jesus surely didn't say these things only once! Many and varying performances of similar material may lead to similar but different texts. Which saying is the "original," Matthew's or Luke's? We don't know which one occurred first, and it probably doesn't matter. Because the audience and situation are different each time, each one is "original," and yet each performance is related because it is the same Jesus who says them and because the sayings and point are so similar. If they reflect two different audiences and two different situations, they are both originals.[13]

Scene 7: *A small group is gathered at the foot of one of the crosses at the crest of the hill outside Jerusalem. There is a sign over the cross that none of them can read. They know it is written in Hebrew, Latin, and Greek. They ask one of the Roman guards what the sign says. He says, "Jesus of Nazareth, King of the Jews."*

Who is the performer in the scene? Is it Pilate, the Roman governor of Judea, who ordered these words be written? Is it the scribe who engraved the text of the sign? Is it the centurion who read it? Or, are they all performers in different ways for different audiences? The audience is more than this small group, but everyone who passes by—and especially those who might aspire to have the title "King of the Jews." It functions as a warning, a threat, to those people! But to Christ-followers after the resurrection, the text of the sign continues to be performed by readers of Matthew, Mark, Luke, or John's Gospel.[14] For these audiences, the sign is less threat than irony: the performance of the Gospels leads them to conclude that the sign tells the truth. Jesus is the promised King.

Scene 8: *A group of women have gathered in the home of Mary from Magdala. They have heard she and a few other women were the first ones at the tomb of Jesus, and that Mary saw messengers who must have been from heaven. They told her that Jesus was alive! As she has done for weeks, she insists on telling the story from the beginning, to build up to the dramatic experience she had at the tomb and encourage her audience to tell the story to others. "This is the*

13. On the multiple performances that led to what we now call the "Sermon on the Mount" and the "Sermon on the Plain," see the suggestion first by George Kennedy, *New Testament Interpretation through Rhetorical Criticism* (Chapel Hill: University of North Carolina Press, 1984), 68.

14. Matt 27:37; Mark 15:26; Luke 23:38; John 19:19–20. Note four slightly different performances of the inscription. Kelly R. Iverson notes that Mark as storyteller juxtaposes mockery and confession in a similar way in the centurion's confession that Jesus is the "Son of God." Iverson, "A Centurion's 'Confession': A Performance-Critical Analysis of Mark 15:39," *Journal of Biblical Literature* 130, no. 2 (2011): 329–50.

beginning of the Good News of Jesus Christ, the Son of God. As it is written in the prophet Isaiah, 'See, I am sending my messenger ahead of you. . . .'"

Mary Magdalene, along with other women who followed Jesus, are uniquely privileged to be the witnesses of the empty tomb and the angelic messengers who explain that Jesus is alive (see, for example, Mark 16:1–8). The only way we could know these things today is because they told the story! In other words, they performed the story for others. Most likely, they didn't perform it once but many times as people wanted to hear what they saw—and what it means. As people asked Mary what Jesus' resurrection means, it would be natural for her to tell the story from the beginning. She has no text but her memory. Through her memory of her experiences and hearing others tell stories about Jesus, she could expand or contract the length of the story based on the time available and the audience's responses. By telling the story many times, she sharpens her language to be the most economical for the greatest impact on her audience. Although long before Mark wrote his version, Mary's telling may have been similar to Mark's Gospel. Mark, the shortest of the Gospels, can be told in about seventy-five minutes and contains many common storytelling features. Also, the earliest versions of Mark end with the humble confession that the women said nothing to anyone because they were afraid. As Mary ends the story, she demonstrates that she has overcome her fear. How that must have encouraged her audience to overcome their fear to tell the story to others![15]

Scene 9: *"Where do the Judeans go to pray?" "Down by the river," says everyone in the Roman colony of Philippi. On the Sabbath, Paul and his companions find a few women, mostly from out of town, who gather to pray and to hear what Torah can be recited from memory, and perhaps to sing a psalm. Always hospitable, the group gives Paul an opportunity to speak. He stands and begins to gesture, saying that Jesus is the fulfillment of the promise*

15. See Antoinette Clark Wire's argument that Mark's Gospel may have been told by Mary and the other women in *The Case for Mark Composed in Performance* (Eugene, OR: Cascade, 2011), 183–86. See also Joanna Dewey, "The Survival of Mark's Gospel: A Good Story?," *Journal of Biblical Literature* 123, no. 3 (Fall 2004): 495–507.

to Abraham and Sarah, the Messiah promised to David's house, the one whom God raised from the dead, the one who sets them free from sins. One woman, Lydia, a merchant from the city of Thyatira across the Aegean Sea in Asia Minor, invites Paul to tell about Jesus to her family. She and her household are baptized and invite Paul and his company to stay in her home while they are in Philippi.[16]

In Acts 16:11–15, Luke portrays Paul as performing the story of Jesus and its significance for a group of Jewish women (and perhaps Gentiles who are interested in Judaism). There is no building—only a familiar meeting place on the bank of a river, perhaps where there is ample shade as well as water and quiet. Luke does not tell us the words he used in Philippi, but it is unlikely he used a manuscript for his speech. Paul spoke before the synagogue in Antioch of Pisidia without any script (Acts 13:13–52), but Luke seems to show that speech to be a model of the kind of speeches Paul gave. In front of a Jewish audience, Paul usually tells the story of Jesus by telling the story of Israel. He begins with the exodus from slavery in Egypt, while emphasizing their identity as descendants of Abraham and Sarah. He has no written text, only his memories of the stories of God's people that we now know in the Hebrew Bible. How does the audience respond? One listener, Lydia, is persuaded to become a Christ-follower and her whole household is baptized. Performance leads to changed identity!

Scene 10: *While Paul was in Achaia, he remembered warmly his time with believers to the north in the city of Thessaloniki—about 160 kilometers (about a hundred miles) west of Philippi. He heard through the gossip network that they had a number of anxieties and questions. He wants to visit them, but feels compelled to stay in Achaia. He sent Timothy to encourage and teach them, but still there are questions and concerns. So, the next best thing to being there is to send a letter. Paul, Silvanus, and Timothy talk through the contents of the letter. They want it to be read to the whole Christian community. How will each person hear it? After discussion, Silvanus makes a draft of the letter by using*

16. I am assuming that Luke understands Paul's message in this "place of prayer" to follow the pattern established in Acts 13:13–52. On the "Law and Prophets" perhaps referring to the Psalms as "prophetic," see Barr, *Writing on the Tablet*, 265–66.

a wooden stylus to make impressions in a wax tablet. He reads back what has been dictated and they make changes in the wax. When they are satisfied with how it sounds, Silvanus copies the letter from the wax using ink on a piece of papyrus.[17]

Paul, Silvanus, and Timothy are a performance trio shaping a text that is intended to be read aloud to a group. Silvanus, as the scribe in this scene, is the first audience who takes the discussion and distills the phrases and ideas into successive drafts until the group agrees with the wording and tone of the letter we now call "First Thessalonians." Is each draft of the letter a separate performance? Another person will be the performer who appears before the congregation in Thessaloniki to read the letter aloud and most likely answer questions from the congregation to clarify its meaning.[18]

Scene 11: *Everybody needs to eat, and we feel like we belong when we eat with others. The Greeks had the tradition of telling stories or sharing a poem or a speech after the meal when the food was digesting and the wine was still flowing. Jews and later Christians didn't like the prayers and sips of wine dedicated to Dionysius and Zeus, so they had their own stories, poems, and speeches and their own prayers to offer. As Justin explains Christianity to non-Christians, he says that Christians gather once a week on Sunday and had their readings and prayers first before the meal:*

> *The recollections of the apostles or the writings of the prophets are read, as long as there is time. When the reader has finished, the president of the assembly speaks to us; he urges everyone to imitate the examples of virtue we have heard in the readings. Then we all stand up together and pray. On the conclusion of our prayer, bread and wine and water are brought forward. The president offers*

17. I arbitrarily chose Silvanus as the scribe, but it could be an unnamed amanuensis ("one who takes dictation"). On reading the letter before the community, see 1 Thess 5:27.
18. On the composition of letters, see Hans-Josef Klauck, *Ancient Letters and the New Testament* (Waco, TX: Baylor University Press, 2006). On the reading and explanation of the letter, see Margaret M. Mitchell, "New Testament Envoys in the Context of Greco-Roman Diplomatic and Epistolary Conventions: The Example of Timothy and Titus," *Journal of Biblical Literature* 111, no. 4 (Winter 1992): 641–62. On the performance of Paul's letters, see Lee A. Johnson, "Paul's Epistolary Presence in Corinth: A New Look at Robert W. Funk's Apostolic Parousia," *The Catholic Biblical Quarterly* 68, no. 3 (July 2006): 481–501; Pieter J. J. Botha, *Orality and Literacy in Early Christianity* (Eugene, OR: Cascade, 2012); and Bernhard Oestreich, *Performanzkritik der Paulusbriefe* (Tübingen: Mohr Siebeck, 2012).

> *prayers and gives thanks to the best of his ability, and the people give assent by saying, "Amen."*[19]

After everyone had received the bread and wine mixed with water, some of the leaders took bread and wine to those who were absent.

As with some of the others we've described, this scene from Justin Martyr's *First Apology* (c. 150 CE) is a performance within a performance. Justin performs what Christians perform when they gather. In Justin's performance, the point is to show nonbelievers that Christian practice is not strange, but comparable with Greek meals where food and traditional readings bond people together in common identity.

The embedded performance echoes other scenes we have discussed: the reading of memories before a group with interpretation for the present audience. The sharing of food after the time of readings and prayers may recall the serving of food after Ezra read the Law. This combination of food with performance is a common theme—and a potent one that welds people together in common identity and purpose. When the reader shares the memories of the apostles and prophets, it is not simply information. The performance and its interpretation by the "president of the assembly" is expected to transform the audience's behavior.

Scene 12: *It is a Wednesday night in January in Arizona, and I stand on a stage in front of about 250 mostly comfortable middle- to upper-class people, who have gathered at their church to hear me explain what the book of Revelation means. I have just finished saying that we can't begin to understand the book of Revelation until we've had an experience of the book of Revelation. I have asked them to imagine they are representatives from seven congregations who have gathered to hear a messenger share the visions given to a prophet named John. I stand for a moment silently, with a scroll rolled up in my hand. I hold the scroll high over my head and say, "This is a revelation of Jesus Christ, which God gave him to show his slaves what must happen soon. . . ."*

This scene is not imagined, but a brief description of my

19. Justin Martyr, *First Apology* 66–67.

performance of the book of Revelation in January 2014. The "text" is my translation of the book of Revelation that I memorized as well as the scroll that I use as a prop (which really is a scroll of the Greek text of Revelation). In chapter 4 of this book, I will be discussing this performance and others that illuminate the process and payoff of biblical performance criticism.

Initial Reflections

The twelve scenes described above portray different kinds of performers, audiences, interactions, texts, and situations. These scenes are brief and incomplete, but evocative of the issues this book addresses. Here are some summary comments to consider with your own reflections.

In some scenes, the performer and audience are obvious. The audience has chosen to give attention to the performer and, in many cases, power. The power is important to note: when an audience allows themselves to be transformed by the performance, they yield power to the performer. In some cases, such as the scene with the father and son, the distinction between performer and audience is more fluid, with roles reversing or with give and take, which suggests power is shared more flexibly. But in other cases, the performer is performing for a scribe, such as a letter writer or engraver, who prepares a text for a different audience in a different time, place, and situation. The written text becomes somewhat independent of the initial performer because when it is performed again something will be different, the performer, the audience, and/or the situation. Everything may be changed by these differences, even the meaning and impact of the text! But the written text carries with it the initial act of power that caused its creation. Paul's letter to the Thessalonians carries his claim to authority. The inscription over Jesus' head reminds inescapably every further performer of Pilate's (and Rome's) power. The scroll I hold up claims authority as Jesus' revelation through John.

The bodies of the performer and audience are important in almost every scene: the posture of father and son as they recall the commandments. The father's nod of acceptance. The singers' and musicians' posture as they perform. Isaiah's naked body. Ezra's standing to read. The audience standing when they see the scroll, bowing to pray, and weeping. The food shared, some hunger satisfied. Paul's gestures as he speaks. The body language of the audience. *Each performance is an embodied experience.*

Every performance *expects* some kind of response by the audience and responses happen even during the performance. The father expects his son to respond with the Ten Commandments, and his son interrupts the lesson with a question. Isaiah expects his nakedness and his explanation to shake a complacent, overconfident ruling class to abandon their alliance with Egypt and Ethiopia. Ezra and other leaders expect to pause the reading, explain it, and take questions. After reading the recollections of the apostles, the president expects Christians to imitate their virtues. In some cases, the audience is expected to become performers for a new audience: Heman's family and singers are first taught as audience but become performers. Mary Magdalene performs the story of Jesus for others and then expects them to become performers.

What is the "text"? When Ezra reads the Law, Jesus reads Isaiah, or the lector reads the recollections of the apostles, there is a written text to be referenced by the reader and seen by the audience. But for many performances, there is no written text present, only the memory of the performer. The focus on memory is clear even when the text is present, for example, "the recollections of the apostles." Even without a physical text, some performances will be similar to other performances in every respect, such as the father's response to his son may resemble the responses of other fathers. Other performances may rearrange material, such as Jesus reordering and tweaking his sayings and stories for different audiences. The text of these performance events would not be written until years later, and perhaps in very different circumstances. Our notions of "text" are not as fixed as we think, but are always dependent on memory and the performances of memory in specific situations.

The situation of a specific performance seems to determine the impact of a performance. A recitation of the Ten Commandments can take on one meaning in a time of peace and another in a time of conflict. Isaiah's words about the Spirit of the Lord can mean the joy of a prophet announcing release from exile or a claim that Jesus is the long-promised King. The inscription, "Jesus of Nazareth, King of the Jews," can mean a threat to those with royal aspiration or an ironic truth that Jesus really is King. The particular words performed are insufficient to decide what they mean for a specific audience. More information about the situation is needed to make sense of them.

The Plan of This Book

The focus of this book is insights from performance criticism, but we also need to present the why, what, and how of biblical performance criticism (chapter 2). Performance criticism offers keen insights into the Bible. It helps explain what is in the Bible and how the Bible is used. Chapters 3 and 4 are concrete examples of how it works. In chapter 3, we examine the Hebrew prophet Habakkuk and see how his prophecies make more sense if we view them as performances. Chapter 4 shares what I have learned about the book of Revelation by performing it with various audiences. Chapter 5 describes ten insights that I have learned from practicing performance criticism. In chapter 6, we will describe the challenges and considerations facing this young way of understanding the Bible.

2

What Is Biblical Performance Criticism?

To describe biblical performance criticism, I start by explaining how human beings communicate. Performance criticism analyzes and practices certain kinds of communication, specifically repeated behaviors for an audience. Inquiry, imagination, and intervention are three aspects of a performance and its analysis. Biblical performance criticism is the analysis and practice of performances of biblical traditions. The basic method of biblical performance criticism is to prepare, internalize, and perform a biblical text. Although it may make it sound like a step-by-step process, performance criticism is really more circular and interrelated, like nodes on a network that influence each other rather than a recipe to follow.

How Do Humans Communicate?

All interpretation of the Bible, and interpretation in general, depends on a theory of how human beings communicate. Biblical performance criticism is indebted to linguists—scholars of language—who have revised the way we think of language and communication. We now understand that human communication works through the interaction of a *speaker*, *signs* (which may include words spoken or written, such as in a "text"), an *audience*, and their *situation*—the four elements of a performance introduced in the last chapter.

For much of the last three hundred years, language has been thought of as a code to be deciphered. Some people read the Bible this way: if we only knew the proper translation or meaning of a word, there would be no controversy about what it "means." From a code mindset, we say, "The Bible says it, I believe it," as if the fixed print on the page should translate into a fixed meaning for everyone reading it. If language was a code, that might be true: a code means the same thing whenever or wherever it's decoded and isn't affected by the person decoding it. When Little Orphan Annie sends a message in code over the radio, any hearers who have a decoder ring are able to decode it, for example, to represent "Eat your Ovaltine." Yet, even if you can decode who Little Orphan Annie is, what a "decoder ring" is, and what "Ovaltine" is, deciphering these words doesn't answer why you should care. If you didn't grow up in the 1940s, have not seen the 1983 movie *A Christmas Story*, or saw it but don't remember it, these references will seem strange and this paragraph difficult to understand. If you know what I'm talking about, you may have smiled or even chuckled. How could simply decoding these words do all that? There has to be more than coding and decoding to explain how we communicate.

The study of human communication over the last century has shown that language is best understood as a system of *signs* and not codes.[1] Certainly, there is a part of language that functions like a code, but this inadequately explains the way language really works. Like a "one-way" traffic sign on the street, words point a hearer or reader toward the intended effect. By "signs" we mean more than words. Signs may include noises, tone, gestures, facial expressions, and movement that

1. This formulation is usually credited to Swiss linguist Ferdinand de Saussure, whose lectures between 1907 and 1911 were collected as a book titled *Course in General Linguistics* (original French title: *Cours de linguistique générale*). There are many different schools of linguistics but they largely agree with the presentation here. For an introduction to the convergences and diversity of thought, see *The Handbook of Linguistics*, ed. Mark Aronoff and Janie Rees-Miller (Oxford: Wiley-Blackwell, 2003). The following discussion is based on relevance theory (RT) as described in Dan Sperber and Deidre Wilson, *Relevance: Communication and Cognition*, 2d ed. (Oxford: Wiley-Blackwell, 1996), because RT explains the communication process clearly and elegantly.

guide a hearer. Consider the way American Sign Language (ASL) works to communicate without sound. ASL is a language—a system of signs—that is used by "speakers" to lead "hearers" to chosen effects.

Thinking of communication in terms of signs takes into account the way words and other signs function differently depending on the situation and audience. Signs cannot be considered apart from the space and time in which they function. Signs are interpreted by an audience that draws on their observations, ideas, imagination, and, perhaps most importantly, their memory to interpret the signs.

Imagine a one-way traffic sign. When you think of it, you are remembering a sign you have seen before and, if you are a driver, your experience of one on the street. You may also recall the experience of driving the wrong way on a one-way street and the emotions of embarrassment or fear that accompanied the experience. That was not my intended effect in originally mentioning it, but the thought may have come to mind especially since I brought it up. Understanding the sign depends not only on decoding the words *one* and *way* and the pointing arrow, but also the larger situation of the street, automobiles, and the direction of travel. It may trigger other memories. The communication depends on not only the sign (created by some "author") but also the audience (especially the audience's memory) and the situation in which the sign is found. The intended effect is that drivers will direct their vehicles to travel in the direction of the arrow. The audience's memories may supply meanings beyond the intended effect of the sign's author.

Imagine a one-way sign out in the middle of a green field with cows calmly grazing nearby. What does this sign mean now? The cows are directed to go "one way"? For some, it would be humorous. Others may be offended, thinking the sign was stolen. A code model of human communication is unable to explain humor, irony, metaphor, or responses by different audiences. On an advertisement for milk, a picture of cows and a one-way sign in a field may try to persuade people that there is only one way: "Buy Milk." On publicity for an organic dairy, it may be suggesting that organic farming is the "one way." Human communication depends on the interaction of speaker, signs, audience, and situation, and not on some fixed "meaning" of the words.

Recall the first scene from the last chapter: a father and a son beneath a tree practicing the Ten Commandments. The son asks, "Why do we do this?" How do we explain the father's sigh in response to this question? A code model of communication would say that the father decodes the pronoun "this" to refer to the activity of reciting the commandments out loud, "we" to refer either to the father and son or the larger cultural activity of recitation, and "why" to be a question of purpose. In other words, the father decodes the question to ask, "What is the purpose of my reciting the commandments to you?" But how is a sigh a response to this question? The code model is unable to explain.

Most readers of this scene, however, would have no problem imagining why a father would sigh to his son's request. Even if you are not a father or a son, you probably have enough experience (i.e., memories) of children frustrated with their parents' tedious requests to imagine the tone of the question, "Why do we do this?" We can imagine many different ways the question could be asked: (1) "*Why* do we do this?," with a bit of a whine indicating the *why* is to communicate, "I think this is boring"; (2) "Why do *we* do this?," implying with the *we* that this kind of activity is fine for other fathers and sons but not us; or (3) "Why do we do *this*?" suggesting that he would much rather be playing basketball. In all these cases, the sigh of the father makes sense: he acknowledges that the son is bored or would rather be doing something else.

In the discussion of this scene in the last chapter, however, I suggested an alternative explanation that a modern reader may not consider. In a situation of persecution of Jews who publicly practice their faith, the son's question may be, "Why do we do *this*?," implying that the activity is dangerous. Someone may see and report them. They could be arrested. The sigh communicates that the father recognizes his son's fear. Even in this case, the sigh of the father makes sense as communicating his acknowledgment of his son's *emotion* and not the content of his question. We can't say what that emotion is without more information about the son's tone or the larger situation.

We tend to choose the interpretation that requires the least effort while still explaining the signs that the speaker has chosen. Interpreting the son's question as an expression of fear takes more effort because it requires more information. It is much easier and quicker for a reader to conclude that the son is being whiny because we have prior memories of whiny children (perhaps even of being one) and can access them easily. To conclude that the son is talking about other children reciting the commandments or that he'd rather play basketball would take more effort to access more information. If the son thought his father would have difficulty understanding that he'd rather play basketball, he would have been more explicit and said, "Why do we do this? I'd rather play basketball." The father would not have to work as hard to decide what was meant.

In other words, there is a trade-off of effort for effects. Speakers and authors will naturally try to choose the signs they think will most effectively influence their audience toward desired conclusions.[2] Hearers and readers will naturally select the first meaning that explains the signs in the situation. Hearers of the same words in a new situation, however, may find it difficult or even impossible to experience the intended effects.

This is why reading the Bible can be very difficult for us. The speakers and authors that lie behind what we now call the Bible chose words in Hebrew, Aramaic, and Greek that they thought would have the most effective impact on their audiences for the least amount of the audiences' effort. We try to understand ancient audiences as best we can. We try to reconstruct the situations around those audiences and the kind of impact the texts may have had, but this takes a great deal of effort (which is why we will always need more PhDs in biblical studies, archaeology, cultural anthropology, and so on). We keep translating the Bible in new ways in order to lower the effort that new audiences have to expend to experience its impact. In this way,

2. This is the primary insight of relevance theory.

each translation is a new communication event: a translator producing words intended to have an impact on an audience in a particular language and culture. The point of these examples is to demonstrate that human communication involves a speaker/author who creates signs intended for some effect on an audience in a concrete situation. Some key points:

- Language is a *system of signs.* Words are not codes but signs that a speaker uses to guide an audience toward an intended effect. Possible signs include more than spoken and written words. Signs also include tone, gestures, facial expressions, and movement. Since the Bible comes to us in writing, it is often limited by the media (written or printed words on a page). But when the Bible is re-presented in other media (such as an embodied reading, audio recording, video recording, or hyperlinked text[3] on the Internet), a more diverse set of signs is available to guide an audience to effects. (We will say more about media in the discussion of performance criticism below.)
- Human communication is *inferential.* Audiences use their memories, ideas, observations, and imagination to infer the meaning of the signs in their situation. The signs in themselves are always incomplete. For example, the father has to combine the son's words with his memories and the situation to determine their meaning. The reader almost automatically connects the son's words with their experience of whiny children (or some other information) to decide what is meant. This means readers/hearers of the Bible will always need additional information outside the text in order for it to have an impact.
- We can speak of *intended meaning* because the attempt to communicate brings an assumption that there is some intended effect. The speaker/author assumes their signs will lead to these

3. Hyperlinked texts allow for nonlinear experiences of a text and the possibility for non-memory-based indexing and encyclopedic lookup. For example, I don't have to remember when Augustus Caesar ruled when reading Luke 2; I can click on a link that will lead me to an article on Augustus.

effects. At the same time, it may require too much effort for some audiences to discover what that intended effect was. By interpreting the Bible within this theory of human communication, we have a basis for talking about the author's intention. At the same time, we admit that the intended effects may not be significant to modern readers in the same way as for ancient readers and that the effort may be too great for us to conclude confidently what those intentions were.

- *Unintended effects* are often a part of human communication. While some effects may be intended by the speaker/author, other effects are the product of new inferences the audience makes because of different memories or information. For example, mentioning a one-way sign may cause unintended embarrassment for some hearers. In interpreting the Bible, not all effects that an audience experiences may have been intended by the authors. This helps us admit that even though something is meaningful to us, the author may not have intended it. Likewise, when we are re-presenting the Bible to new audiences, new effects are inevitable and perhaps even desirable. For example, one effect of reading a Bible passage in a synagogue or church may be a feeling of reverence unrelated to the content.
- *Memory* and *imagination* are required in human communication, and often in combination. An audience unconsciously draws on memories to make sense of the signs. They also use imagination to fill in the picture that is presented by the signs. When we are told that a father and son are sitting beneath a tree, we will draw from our memories of trees and places where a father and son might sit. If we think of this as a "biblical scene," we may draw on our imagination of the kind of clothes "Bible characters" wear (probably based on memories of Hollywood productions of Bible stories).

What Is Performance?

The word *performance* evokes a number of thoughts and feelings, depending on the audience and the situation. When we talk about a performance of *The Sound of Music*, it evokes memories of the experiences of actors and actresses playing roles, singing and speaking lines internalized and embodied as if the actor had become the character.

In other situations, we use the word *performance* pejoratively, suggesting that a person is inauthentic or overly emotional. Some may refer to the "performance" of a politician, implying that the politician is only acting and doesn't really believe what they are saying. We may leave a family gathering, shaking our head at the "performance" of an aunt who threw a fit.

What comes to mind with the phrase, "performing the Bible"? The Bible is not usually performed, except in Hollywood. It is usually *read* in synagogues, churches, and homes. When I tell people that I am going to perform part of the Bible, some will try to clarify, "Oh, you mean act it out?" Others will question the appropriateness of "performing" the Bible, suggesting that it would be inauthentic or overly emotional.

There are many ways to define "performance," but all of them include repeated (and sometimes practiced) behaviors for some kind of audience. Richard Schechner, one of the pioneers of performance studies, calls these "restored behaviors," defined as "Physical, verbal, or virtual actions that are not-for-the-first time; that are prepared or rehearsed. A person may not be aware that she is performing a strip of restored behavior. Also referred to as twice-behaved behavior."[4] The scene of father and son practicing the Ten Commandments is a not-for-the-first-time behavior. In part, it is because of the repetition that the son questions the behavior, "Why do we do this?" This, too, is part of a larger pattern of repeated behavior that Deuteronomy reflects and anticipates. The point is that the son and the father each are performers. A recitation of even one of the Ten Commandments is a performance. The father's response to the son's question is also a performance, repeating traditional responses even if in a new situation and even if a physical text is absent.

The second scene in chapter 1 showed the priest Heman teaching his

4. Richard Schechner, *Performance Studies: An Introduction*, 3d ed. (London: Routledge, 2013), 29.

children and musicians (from 1 Chronicles 25). As noted earlier, this is more familiarly thought of as performance perhaps because of the music. But why is this? Why would we think a performance of music in the temple more a "performance" than a son reciting commandments to a father?

One benefit of using the word *performance* is that the term itself is contested. It brings us into the real but often ignored contest for culture, power, and identity. Each group of people negotiates with other groups in society over what is culturally appropriate, who makes decisions, and how identity is shaped. Marvin Carlson argues that we will never be able to agree on a definition for the word *performance* because, at its heart, the term points at the human jockeying to label some behaviors as appropriate and others not appropriate.

> The recognition that our lives are structured according to repeated and socially sanctioned modes of behavior raises the possibility that all human activity could potentially be considered as "performance," or at least all activity carried out with a consciousness of itself. . . . Viewing performance as an essentially contested concept warns us against seeking some over-arching semantic field to cover such seemingly disparate usages as the performance of an actor, of a schoolchild, of an automobile.[5]

We think a performance of music is an appropriate use of the word *performance* but less so a son repeating the commandments to a father because of the way Western cultures separate "entertainment" from more "serious" modes of expression. Other cultures may think differently. As Carlson observes, our lives are "structured according to repeated and socially sanctioned modes of behavior."

The word *performance* brings a focus on *embodiment, power relations,* and *identity*. Socially patterned behavior, such as reciting commandments and singing a psalm response, uses signs (remember that the term *signs* includes more than words) to embody culture, exercise power relations, and establish identity. Consider scene 3 from chapter

5. Marvin Carlson, *Performance: A Critical Introduction,* 2d ed. (London: Routledge, 2004), 4–5. Interestingly, Carlson does speak favorably of Richard Bauman's definition: "all performance involves a consciousness of doubleness, according to which the actual execution of an action is placed in mental comparison with a potential, an ideal, or a remembered original model of that action" (5).

1: Isaiah prophesied while naked to demonstrate that an alliance with Egypt and Ethiopia was futile against Assyria. Isaiah was not simply naked to illustrate the figurative nakedness of Judah's policy; he embodied a set of values that opposed the ruling values. In other words, he disregarded the accepted value of being clothed in public to devalue bodily the king's policy. He embodied his prediction that the rulers would become naked as a result of disregarding the God of Israel. "Culture" refers to the shared system of signs that a group uses to interact, express values, and pattern behaviors. Therefore, the first thing performance does is to *embody culture* (possibly to counter the dominant culture).

The second thing performance does is to *exercise power relationships.* If we understand that power is always relational, an influence granted by one person or group to another person or group, then all human communication takes place within power relations. To perform is to be granted a certain kind of power over the audience. To authorize a performance is to exercise power over the performer and an audience. Take, for example, the father and son and the commandments. The son yields to his father's request to recite the commandments. This is an exercise of power. The son, however, shifts the power dynamic by stopping the recital to ask, "Why?" The question reverses the power dynamic: the father is asked to become the performer. The father's sigh and nod, in part, represent his acceptance of his son's influence. In the case of Isaiah's prophecy, he has been authorized by the king as a court prophet; the king has yielded power to Isaiah, which gives him a platform for his prophecy. It is likely this authorization protected Isaiah from being jailed or worse for three years of naked performance. In each of these cases, to call these repeated behaviors "performance" helps illuminate that they exercise power relationships.

Third, performance *establishes identity.* "Performance" is a contested term because it presents different ways of representing oneself. In the theater, taking on a role is deemed acceptable. But isn't the father also asking the son to take on a role by repeating the Ten Commandments? He is asking his son not only to repeat them by rote, but to allow his behavior, thoughts, and attitudes to be transformed by the performance. The son's question raises the question of identity to his father. "Why do we do this?" is answered by "This is who we are." Performance shapes identity and allows for performer and audience to change identities, even if only temporarily, in the performance.

To summarize, "performance" provides a fitting term for analyzing biblical passages. Biblical passages are used in not-for-the-first-time behaviors such as the scenes described in chapter 1. Each is representative of repeated, patterned behaviors. Consider how the Bible is used today: each use of the Bible, whether in synagogue, church, academy, or home, is in some way a repeated behavior. A quotation of a verse, an allusion to a passage, a reading of a chapter, or a dramatization of a book—these are all performances. Biblical passages are used to embody culture, exercise power relations, and establish identity.

What Is Performance Criticism?

Simply put, performance criticism is the *analysis and practice of performance.* We are using "performance criticism" and "performance studies" interchangeably, although "criticism" may imply that we can be objective about the performance, and that is not what we mean. The insight here is that scholarship and performance may be distinguished but are inseparable. The performer is an analyst and the analyst is a performer. Dwight Conquergood writes, "The ongoing challenge of performance studies is to refuse and supersede this deeply entrenched division of labor, apartheid of knowledge, that plays out inside the academy as the difference between thinking and doing, interpreting and making, conceptualizing and creating. The division of labor between theory and practice, abstraction and embodiment, is an arbitrary and rigged choice, and, like all binarisms, it is booby-trapped."[6] The performance critic stands at a distance to analyze only within a larger movement between performance and reflection on

6. Dwight Conquergood, "Performance Studies: Interventions and Radical Research," *The Drama Review* 46, no. 2 (Summer 2002): 145–56, at 153.

performance. The façade of scholarly objectivity has disintegrated under the last half century of growing self-awareness. Performance criticism offers a way to reunite analysis and practice. In terms of biblical performance criticism, in which the texts of the Bible are the object of reflection and the source of performance material, this is a call for scholars to become performers of biblical and extra-biblical texts (more about this in chapter 5).

The performance critic does not stand alone. Performance criticism is essentially and radically interdisciplinary and communal. Since we as human beings communicate using signs that are culturally shaped, our performances and reflections on performance depend on the community in which we live and interpret our experiences. Since our signs are related to every aspect of human life, many disciplines that have been historically divided and compartmentalized are brought together in conversation. D. Soyini Madison and Judith Hamera write in their introduction to the *Sage Handbook of Performance Studies*: "Across various academic boundaries, performance is blurring disciplinary distinctions and invoking radically multidisciplinary approaches. From the established disciplines of history, literature, education, sociology, geography, anthropology, political science, and so forth—the rubric of performance has found its way into discussion and debate as a topic of interest and inquiry."[7] For biblical performance criticism, this means embracing the insights of other critical disciplines, such as: historical criticism, archaeology, cultural anthropology, textual criticism, rhetorical criticism, media criticism, translation theory, and narrative criticism.[8]

Conquergood suggests that performance studies can bring together the divided and fragmented scholarly world. He suggests three *i*'s to organize our thinking about performance: imagination, inquiry, and intervention:

7. D. Soyini Madison and Judith Hamera, "Performance Studies at the Intersections," in *The Sage Handbook of Performance Studies*, ed. D. Soyini Madison and Judith Hamera (Thousand Oaks, CA: Sage, 2006), xi–xxv, at xii–xiii.

8. See David Rhoads, "Performance Criticism: An Emerging Methodology in Second Testament Studies—Part II," *Biblical Theology Bulletin* 36, no. 4 (2006): 164–84, for suggestions for how biblical performance criticism reframes these critical methods.

> Performance studies is uniquely suited for the challenge of braiding together disparate and stratified ways of knowing. . . . We can think of performance (1) as a work of *imagination*, as an object of study; (2) as a pragmatics of *inquiry* (both as a model and method), as an optic and operator of research; (3) as a tactics of *intervention*, an alternative space of struggle. . . . Speaking from my home department at Northwestern [University], we often refer to the three *a*'s of performance studies: artistry, analysis, activism. Or to change the alliteration, a commitment to the three *c*'s of performance studies: creativity, critique, citizenship (civic struggles for social justice).[9]

We can envision performance criticism as engaging in a circular process, moving from imagination to inquiry to intervention and back to imagination.

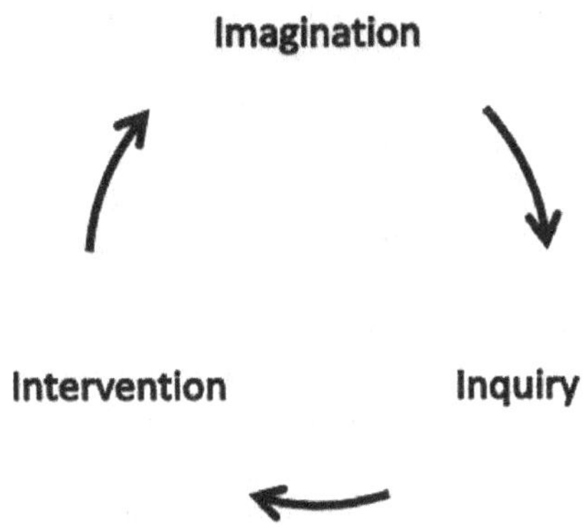

Performance is a work of *imagination* that synthesizes memories, values, attitudes, and perceptions about the audience, society, and the cosmos. Performance is *inquiry* that steps back to a place of critical distance in order to analyze culture, power, and identity. By embodying alternative ways of knowing and being, performance is an *intervention* into culture, power relations, and identity that leads back

9. Conquergood, "Performance Studies," 152; emphasis in the original.

into imagination and re-performance.[10] With this process in mind, we turn to how performance criticism may be applied to biblical texts.

What Is Biblical Performance Criticism?

The phrase "biblical performance criticism" emerged out of the work of "The Bible in Ancient and Modern Media" section of the Society of Biblical Literature. A two-part article by David Rhoads, titled "Performance Criticism: An Emerging Methodology in Second Testament Studies," pointed in the direction that many performers and scholars have followed. I quote extensively from his article to illustrate performance as imagination, inquiry, and intervention:

> The experience of translating, memorizing, and performing these works has placed me in a fresh medium, an entirely different relationship with these texts than that of a silent reader and even quite distinct from the experience of hearers in an audience. . . . By taking on the persona/voice of the narrator or speaker in a text, I enter the world of the text, grasp it as a whole, reveal this world progressively in a temporal sequence, attend to every detail, and gain an immediate experience of its rhetoric as a performer seeking to have an impact on an audience. I have gotten in touch with the emotive and kinetic dimensions of the text in ways I would not otherwise have been aware. As I practice performance, the words come off the page and become sounds in my inner hearing before I speak. Eventually, I am no longer seeing words on a page or anticipating sounds in my head. Rather, I imagine the scenes in my mind and I tell/show what I "see/hear" to a living audience before me. My students who learn texts for performance also speak of the enlivening of their imagination, a new capacity to identify with the different characters, a fresh sense of the emotive dimensions of the texts, and an experience of their rhetorical power.

10. Rhoads suggests that biblical performance criticism has three approaches: (1) imagining performance events, (2) reorienting New Testament methods, and (3) performing as a method of interpreting. I am redistributing these three approaches under Conquergood's rubric of inquiry, imagination, and intervention. See David Rhoads, "What Is Performance Criticism?," in *The Bible in Ancient and Modern Media: Story and Performance*, ed. Holly E. Hearon and Philip Ruge-Jones (Eugene, OR: Cascade, 2009), 83–100. Jeanette Mathews, in *Performing Habakkuk: Faithful Re-Enactment in the Midst of Crisis* (Eugene, OR: Wipf & Stock, 2012), 27–35, suggests five themes that roughly correlate with this description of imagination, inquiry, and intervention: self-reflexivity (making culture conscious to both performer and viewer; exposing culture for critical reflection), embodiment (whole bodies matter, not just voices or texts), universality (holistic features of communication "applicable to many social, cultural, and artistic phenomena"), process (the process of performance is the focus of inquiry, not just the completion of the event), reenactment (all performance is based on preexisting models).

> The audiences of these performances are also experiencing the text in a fresh medium. When I perform in contemporary settings, people speak of a second naiveté, as though they were experiencing the story or letter for the first time. They comment on the new insights that come from hearing in contrast to reading, how unique it is to experience the whole story/letter at one sitting, how they get drawn into the world of the story, how inflection and tone give fresh meaning to this line or that episode, and how the story/letter/apocalypse impacts them in new ways. There emerges a relationship between performer and audience that assists in the act of interpretation. I have gotten many insights into texts by attending to the responses of these audiences—both during performances and also in discussions afterward. In this way, performing and hearing have become major tools of research for me in the study of the Second Testament. They have become the primary means by which I come to interpret the meaning and rhetoric of a text.
>
> The challenge of performance criticism is to draw these and other strands together to form a coherent discipline that is able to give a comprehensive account of the oral dynamics of performance events in the early church.[11]

These are the reflections of a performer and scholar—one whose performance is informed by years of study and then embodied before audiences. Although imagination is evident in any performance, the performance is also a synthesis of the fruits of prior inquiry. The scenes Rhoads imagines are rich with detail because he has inquired deeply into the biblical text and many other ancient texts, archaeology, comparative anthropology, and other disciplines.

Inquiry, imagination, and intervention correspond to Paul Ricoeur's three ways of reading a text, or three "worlds": the world *behind* the text, the world *of* the text, and the world *in front of* the text.[12] The "world behind the text" refers to the situation out of which an author writes a text for a particular audience. As readers of a text, we catch glimpses and clues of who, what, when, where, and why the author wrote. We have only limited access to this world and a view of it that

11. David Rhoads, "Performance Criticism: An Emerging Methodology in Second Testament Studies—Part I," *Biblical Theology Bulletin* 36, no. 3 (2006): 120–21.
12. Paul Ricoeur, *Hermeneutics and the Human Sciences: Essays on Language, Action and Interpretation*, ed. and trans. J. B. Thompson (London: Cambridge University Press, 1981). For a similar methodology, see Richard W. Swanson's work, for example, *Provoking the Gospel of Mark: A Storyteller's Commentary Year B* (Cleveland: Pilgrim, 2005), 77–80.

is shaped by our own interests and concerns.[13] The text itself does not reveal more than hints to this situation, the author's point of view, and goals. We depend on the disciplines of archaeology, other literature, the historical-critical method, textual criticism, comparative anthropology, form criticism, source criticism, and so on, to reconstruct this world. This is what Rhoads has done through his study of Second Temple Judaism and New Testament in preparing to perform Mark. Likewise, Tom Boomershine's inquiry into the world of Mark's audience is determinative for how he performs Mark's passion and resurrection narrative.[14]

Experiencing a performance of a text creates a world of its own in the performer and audience's imagination, the "world of the text." As Rhoads says, "By taking on the persona/voice of the narrator or speaker in a text, I enter the world of the text . . . ," and the audience "is drawn in" with him. Rhoads imagines the scenes in his mind as he performs, and the audience experiences it "as if for the first time." The words, the gestures, and other signs of the performer create an imaginative world that offers a variation on the "real world," with actors and geographical settings. In performance, the performer becomes someone different—a narrator of a Gospel, for example, or Phoebe reading Paul's letter to a Roman congregation. Audience members become bystanders and sometimes participants in this alternative world created in their imagination. It is this distance between the "world behind the text" and the "world of the text" that gives the performance its power to offer alternative ways of being. Alternative culture, power relations, and identity are imagined, which is why the experience has the power to transform.[15] Narrative criticism

13. Richard Swanson (ibid., 80), renames "the world behind the text" the "Inter-text: The World We Think We Live In," which is helpful because he reminds us this is always a construction of the past situation. However much we strive for our reconstruction to match the data, it will never fully represent "what really happened."

14. Thomas E. Boomershine, *The Messiah of Peace: A Performance-Criticism Commentary on Mark's Passion-Resurrection Narrative* (Eugene, OR: Cascade, 2015). See videos of his performances in Greek and English at http://www.messiahofpeace.com.

15. See Ricoeur, *Hermeneutics*, 112, on this concept, which he calls "distanciation." For an example of how the book of Daniel creates an alternative "literacy," see Jin H. Han, *Daniel's Spiel: Apocalyptic Literacy in the Book of Daniel* (Lanham, MD: University Press of America, 2008).

is helpful to analyze the "world of the text," the way the text creates actors (characters), setting, and point of view.[16]

There is also a "world in front of the text," which is to say, the ways people use texts that may have little to do with the original situations or the alternative world that the performance creates in the imagination. As we have already noted, "meaning" (or, better, "effect") is not made by the text but by the experience of performer, text, and audience in a particular situation. Inevitably, the audience will have experienced other performances, either of this text or others. They will have ideas and expectations for a performance in general, and perhaps even this performer and text. On one hand, a performance is related to other performances that the audience has experienced and similarities reinforce memories of previous experiences. On the other hand, inevitable differences catch the attention of the audience and open up new avenues for understanding. In this way, each performance of a text is a new intervention into a particular audience and a particular situation. For example, many Jews and Christians today experience texts ritually performed in worship. The way of reading biblical texts in worship is based on many, many performances within communities. The thick layers of performance experiences create expectations and effects completely independent of the content of the text itself. For example, consider scene 4 from chapter 1: Ezra reads the Law. When a modern Jewish community hears this scene of Ezra and others reading the Law, they cannot but think of the way that the Torah is read each Shabbat. They don't imagine Ezra "reading" each line in a spoken monotone but, rather, chanting a Torah portion in tones and a manner similar to the performances they have experienced. This image of Ezra as cantor is not cued by the text itself, but by the "world in front of the text" that reflects how the community shapes its culture, power relations, and identity using the text.[17] Oral-tradition studies, memory studies, media studies, redaction

16. Rhetorical criticism and discourse analysis also may be useful to better understand the persuasive and structural strategies of the text.

17. See Swanson, *Provoking the Gospel*, 80, as an example of how the life of the worshiping community shapes the performance of a text.

criticism, reception criticism, feminist criticism, liberationist readings, postcolonial criticism, and so on are helpful to understand better the "world in front of the text."

We can summarize the way performance criticism integrates the insights of many disciplines with the following table:

Aspect of Performance	*Way of Reading a Text*	*Critical Disciplines*
Inquiry	World Behind the Text	Historical-Critical Method
		Archaeology
		Comparative Anthropology
		Form Criticism
		Source Criticism
		Historic Rhetorical Criticism
Imagination	World of the Text	Narrative Criticism
Intervention	World in Front of the Text[18]	Oral-Tradition Studies
		Memory Studies
		Media Studies
		Redaction Criticism
		Reception Criticism
		Canon Criticism
		New Rhetorical Criticism
		Reader-Response Criticism
		Feminist Criticism
		Liberationist Readings
		Postcolonial Criticism

This table is too simplistic, since a performer embodies all of it in performance, integrating all their experiences of a text and critical analysis of it into the performance. Inquiry, imagination, and intervention are each aspects of an inseparable performance, and could each be considered aspects of different approaches to a text.

18. Included here might also be *Wirkungsgeschichte* ("history of influence"), or the study of the impact that a text has on diverse audiences throughout history.

Furthermore, performance criticism is not a linear process but a circular one, or perhaps better thought of as a network of nodes in a system always relating to each other.[19]

Does this also mean that the performance critic needs to be proficient in all these critical methods? No. Someone desiring to begin performance criticism needs only to prepare, internalize, and perform. Over time and with increasing experience with various methods, the performance critic will be enriched by integrating the insights of other disciplines into their process.

Method: How Do I Do It?

The basic method of performance criticism is to *prepare*, to *internalize*, and to *perform*. We will demonstrate the method in the next two chapters, but describe it here.

The first step is to *prepare* a text to perform. A text may be as short as one verse or as long as a whole book of the Bible. Preparation of that text for performance begins with an inquiry into the world behind the text, especially focusing on the media culture. Preparation also includes inquiry into the new audience and situation. Preferably, this step includes a translation that pays attention to the sound and embodiment of the text for a new audience and situation.

The second step is to *internalize* the text and its performance. Performance critics have moved away from using the word *memorization* because it implies rote, word-for-word repetition.[20] "Internalization" means more than learning the words. It means deeply understanding the strategies and structure of the text's ideas and engaging the body, emotions, and imagination. It is learning the text "by heart." The prophets Ezekiel and John of Patmos symbolically "ate" their texts and then embodied it in their prophetic action (Ezek 3:3; Rev 10:10). The performer's face, hands, and body express the

19. For a discussion of systemic thinking in performance criticism see J. A. (Bobby) Loubser, *Oral and Manuscript Culture in the Bible: Studies on the Media Texture of the New Testament—Explorative Hermeneutics* (Eugene, OR: Cascade, 2013), 35–44.

20. See Richard Ward and David Trobisch, *Bringing the Word to Life: Engaging the New Testament through Performing It* (Grand Rapids: Eerdmans, 2013), 70; Rhoads, "Performance Criticism—Part I," 125.

text along with the voice. This should be no surprise, since human communication is not about transmitting codes but balancing desired effects with the effort required of an audience. A performer adjusts the performance of an internalized text in response to audience feedback, including changing words, gestures, intonation, volume, and movement in order to reach the desired effects. Although a text can be performed simply by reading it from the page, internalizing it allows the performer to subtly control the myriad details and better achieve desired effects for the audience.

The third step is to *perform* the text. The performance brings it all together: embodying the text for a group of people. The performance is more than just the words of the text. It begins when the performer walks or stands in front of the group opens their mouth to introduce the experience and set expectations. The performance also includes any kind of concluding remarks, discussion, or audience response. Both introduction and conclusion should be considered carefully for the specific audience and are analyzed as a part of performance criticism.

To call them steps is an oversimplification. When internalizing a text, questions will arise that will force the performance critic back to preparation. After performing a text for an audience, new questions will emerge for inquiry and new issues for internalization. It is perhaps helpful to view it as a circle.

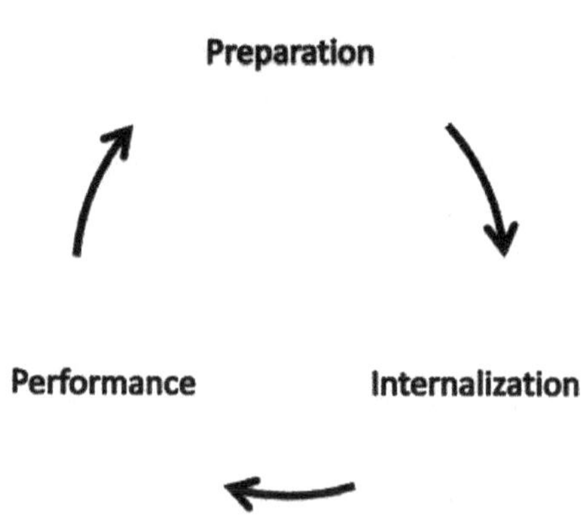

Step 1: Preparation

The first step of performance criticism is *preparation*, which roughly correlates to inquiry. First, the performance critic studies the "*world behind the text*," the situation in which authors wrote the text, with special attention to the media culture. Next, the critic analyzes the "*world of the text*" to understand how the text creates actors (characters) and settings within the imagination. Then, the critic analyzes the "*world in front of the text*," including the expected audience and the contemporary performance situation to choose signs (words, gestures, movement, intonation, and so on) that will maximize the desired effects for the particular audience. Finally, if the performance critic is working with biblical languages, a translation is prepared for the intended audience.

Inquiry: World Behind the Text

As one studies reads the text carefully looking for clues into the "world behind the text," commentaries and studies into the life during biblical times are very helpful. For example, consider scene 5 from chapter 1: Jesus standing in Nazareth to read from the scroll of Isaiah (Luke 4:16–30). What does this passage suggest about the "world behind the text," the performance scenario that Luke assumes would be familiar to his hearers?

Luke reveals something about his world and how he wants to portray Jesus to his audience.[21] He shows Jesus as a scribe, one who embodies the behaviors, attitudes, and values of the group that has access to scrolls and experience reciting them and committing them to memory. Jesus stands to read, and sits to interpret. An attendant hands him a scroll. Jesus himself unrolls the scroll and finds the passage. In all this, Luke identifies Jesus with a group to whom many people yielded

21. Chris Keith argues that Luke is implicitly arguing against Mark's and Matthew's portrayal of Jesus as outside the scribal elite (they portray him as a teacher *and* a manual laborer; see Mark 6:3 // Matt 13:55). By showing Jesus as a member of the scribal elite in Luke 4, Keith asserts that Luke is minimizing the conflict about the source of Jesus' authority with the scribes who hold authority over tradition and its meaning. See Keith, *Jesus against the Scribal Elite: The Origins of the Conflict* (Grand Rapids: Baker Academic, 2014).

power. For those who did not have access to the scrolls of the prophets, who could not spend the time necessary reciting and memorizing them, the scribes (and thus Jesus) had access to God they also did not have. The synagogue leaders yield power to Jesus to allow him to read and teach. When insulted, however, the crowd (and presumably the leaders) revoke the power they yielded and try to throw him off a cliff!

We ask questions to describe further this performance scenario and the culture it assumes. Although important, we shouldn't get too bogged down in questions of historical accuracy, such as whether there was a building referred to as a "synagogue" on such-and-such a street in Nazareth in the early first century CE. The point is that in the performance of Luke's Gospel, he presents the synagogue as reality. By writing it this way, Luke shows that he believes his audience can imagine it with little effort. What would a first-century audience have imagined when they thought of a synagogue in Nazareth? Some questions that might be raised in preparing this passage for performance may include:

- What would a synagogue in a small village like Nazareth look like?
- How many people would be there? What kind of people? (Men only? Landowners?)
- Where would they store scrolls?
- Who would the "attendant" be?
- Who decided on the Isaiah 61 reading? Jesus or someone else? Was this the appointed reading for the day? Why was a Torah portion not read?
- Luke summarizes Jesus' interpretation ("Today this scripture has been fulfilled in your hearing"). Do we have examples of what Luke thinks he might have said and how he said it?
- For example, emotion clearly played a role in the audience's response (amazement, 4:22; rage, 4:28). How did he evoke

amazement in his speaking? What "gracious words came from his mouth"?

With these questions in mind, we access commentaries, archaeological information, and cultural anthropological analysis to gather as much as can be known about this scenario and scenes like it. For example, by consulting a recent book called *Galilee in the Late Second Temple and Mishnaic Period, Volume 1: Life, Culture, and Society*, we learn that a "synagogue" in Galilee probably referred to a gathering in a multipurpose communal building that had been financed by a wealthy family.[22] They were not only used for Sabbath and other religious meetings, but also for political and social gatherings, judicial proceedings, and, in some cases, even contained a facility for ritual baths. Archaeology has shown no religious dimension to most of these buildings: no ark to hold the Torah scroll and no religious art or symbols. Based on evidence from other ancient texts, scholars suggest that these multipurpose buildings were also used as "synagogues" (literally, "a gathering" or "a place of meeting").

One building from the first century that seems to have been specifically built for religious gatherings is the synagogue in Migdal (Magdala) near the Sea of Galilee.[23] It is about thirty-six by thirty-six feet square, perhaps holding a maximum of two hundred people for a village of about four thousand. It has mosaic floors and frescoed walls. It does have chambers for storing scrolls and study. Perhaps most significantly, archaeologists have uncovered a stone possibly used for supporting the Torah scroll when it was being read aloud. It is engraved with symbols from the Jerusalem temple, including a menorah. James Charlesworth and Mordechai Aviam suggest, "most

22. Lee I. Levine, "The Synagogues of Galilee," in *Galilee in the Late Second Temple and Mishnaic Periods, Volume 1: Life, Culture, and Society*, ed. David A. Fiensy and James Riley Strange (Minneapolis: Fortress Press, 2014), 139; David A. Fiensy, "The Galilean Village in the Late Second Temple and Mishnaic Periods," in ibid., 189. See also Anders Runesson, Donald D. Binder, and Birger Olsson, *The Ancient Synagogue from Its Origins to 200 C.E.: A Source Book* (Leiden: Brill, 2008).
23. Ariel Sabar, "Unearthing the World of Jesus," *Scientific American* 49, no. 6 (January/February 2016): 124. For more reports on this site, see http://www.magdalaproject.org/WP/.

likely Jesus taught in it; and conceivably he met Mary Magdalene there."[24]

Nazareth was smaller than Magdala, about ten acres in size and with fewer than two thousand people. Jesus' hometown was exclusively agricultural and it is less likely that they had a building dedicated to religious meetings. People walked out from their house in the village to their fields. It would likely be a small group who gathered, composed mostly of men who had the time and influence to gather for Sabbath (while other Sabbath activities would take place in homes). As our inquiry begins to move toward imagination, we need to imagine a kind of community center, unadorned by anything we might typically find in a house of worship, and a small group gathered there to hear Jesus.

Media Culture

The concept of *media culture* is essential to performance criticism. When analyzing a text, the performance critic asks: What is the media culture assumed by this passage? This inquiry will cause us to reframe biblical texts as produced in a primarily face-to-face culture rather than a primarily print or electronic culture. "Face-to-face" culture is a different way of expressing what other performance and media critics call "primarily oral culture." Before discussing the difference in terminology, I should explain what a "media culture" is.

The medium shapes the communication.[25] For example, in the twenty-first century we have many different choices of means to communicate: face to face, voice-only over phone or Skype, recorded voice, live video chat, recorded video, television, radio, newspaper, book, magazine, e-mail, text, Internet, just to name a few. Each form of media has possibilities and limitations. For example, based on current technology, we can have a high level of quality in a call between one

24. James H. Charlesworth and Mordechai Aviam, "Reconstructing First-Century Galilee," in *Jesus Research: New Methodologies and Perceptions—The Second Princeton-Prague Symposium on Jesus Research, Princeton 2007*, ed. James H. Charlesworth, Brian Rhea, and Petr Pokorny (Grand Rapids: Eerdmans, 2014), 121.

25. See Marshall McLuhan, *Understanding Media: The Extensions of Man* (New York: Mentor, 1964). The presentation here is drawn from insights in Boomershine, Loubser, and Rodríguez.

cell phone and another that allows hearer and speaker in almost any location to detect nuances in tone and volume. Radio provides a medium for a person or group to reach a very large number of people in an area, if hearers have a receiver with power or battery. We wouldn't try to have the nuanced one-on-one conversation over radio that we can have over a cell-phone call. We would use radio to spread ideas ("to perform culture," to use performance-studies terminology) to a large group, not a one-on-one call. (However, Twitter has made it possible to use a cell phone in this way!)

A "media culture" is the set of values, attitudes, and behaviors that a group has developed around their media. For example, cell phones have radically changed the media culture of the twenty-first century, allowing people to be accessible for long-distance voice or text communication in almost any situation. A striking memory for me is climbing to the top of a hill in a beautiful forest of coastal redwoods to find a couple sitting at a picnic bench, sitting across from each other, face to face but staring at their cell phones, fingers flying as they texted others who were not in that forest. They probably used a smaller set of words in their communication, even abbreviations that suggest physical or emotional responses, such as "lol" to indicate they laughed out loud (even if they might not have made a sound). They likely were not discussing the implications of Luke's presentation of Jesus as a scribe because texting limits the kind and content of communication. They sat that way for over a half hour while I hiked around the area. They were in one of the most beautiful places on earth, presumably with someone they cared about, and, from the look in their eyes, they were miles away. These behaviors (texting someone from a remote forest while face to face with someone else) and values (attention to distant persons over present person) were not possible before texting was widely adopted. The media culture has radically changed.

Different media in a culture can compete with each other. I already commented that Twitter has taken over some of the functions of radio; will radio in the future be used for voice or almost only for music? Newspapers and magazines are media in radical transition in the twenty-first century. The ease and lower cost of mass information through Internet outlets (websites, Facebook, etc.) has meant a change in income for these media.

What was the media culture in biblical times? First, it was not uniform over the development of the traditions now represented in the Bible. We think that the earliest traditions represented in the Bible were transmitted face-to-face by memory.[26] We could call this period a time of "purely oral culture," but I think "purely face-to-face culture" is better. "Oral" or even "spoken" abstracts too much from the bodily experience of communication, as if the voice was separable from the body before the days of audio recording devices. Communication before the advent of writing was a face-to-face experience. We have little access as to how these media cultures worked, because all of our evidence of biblical times is written and even historians who reflect on prehistoric times do so from a media culture influenced by writing.

We do have access to evidence of media cultures where memory was supported by writing. Egyptian, Assyrian, Babylonian, Persian, Greek, and later Roman empires increasingly used tablet inscriptions, monumental inscriptions, graffiti, painting on pottery fragments (called ostraca), scrolls, wax tablets, and codices (bound pages rather than a rolled scroll). Each of these media had a supporting culture that influenced the groups that produced biblical texts, even as face-to-face communication was the most common way that traditions were communicated.

In *The Formation of the Hebrew Bible*, David Carr tells the story of the changing media cultures in this way. Stories that shaped culture and identity were passed from one generation to another by people who

26. David Carr, *The Formation of the Hebrew Bible: A New Reconstruction* (London: Oxford University Press, 2011). See also Loubser, *Oral and Manuscript Culture*, 18–30; and Holly Hearon, "The Interplay Between Written and Spoken Word in the Second Testament as Background to the Emergence of Written Gospels," *Oral Tradition* 25, no. 1 (March 2010): 57–74, http://journal.oraltradition.org/issues/25i/hearon. Loubser describes a layering of oral tradition, with the development of scribal culture (beginning with the development of hieroglyphics in Egypt around 2800 BCE), then intermediate manuscript culture (beginning with the spread of Koine Greek with Alexander the Great around 330 BCE), followed by high manuscript culture (the widespread adoption of the codex in the second century CE). Hearon compares the relationship between the written and spoken as the relationship between land and the sea.

had memorized the stories and retold them many times. We should not think these were "written in stone" but, rather, "in the shifting sand of memory."[27] We have Proverbs in written form now, but they contain the kind of material that would have been taught by parents to children even without a physical "text." This is the kind of education-enculturation activity we saw in the scene of the father and son practicing the Ten Commandments. When these traditions are written, they show minor variations because the traditions were repeated many times in different situations by memory. Carr offers a number of examples from Proverbs that suggest that variation in wording between different written proverbs is the result of memory shifts. In each case the *effect* of the verse is identical even if the words used are different. Compare Prov 6:11 to 24:34:

> 6:11 and your poverty will come like a vagabond
> and your need like an armed man.
> 24:34 and your poverty will come, a vagabond
> and your needs like an armed man.[28]

The differences ("like" and the plural "needs") are only a few letters in Hebrew and do not make significant change in the effect of the verse. Or, consider Prov 16:2a, 21:2a, and 12:15a:

> 16:2a all the ways of a man are pure in his eyes
> 21:2a every way of a man is right in his eyes
> 12:15a the way of the fool is right in his eyes[29]

These variations ("all" or "every," "pure" or "right," and even perhaps the more significant variance of "fool" instead of "man") all communicate a basic point about human nature: people rationalize their behavior.

Because of our modern print-media culture, scholars used to explain

27. Carr, *Formation of the Hebrew Bible*, 36.
28. Ibid., 26.
29. Ibid., 27.

these variations by copying changes. In a culture where the printing press almost guarantees that a copy is identical to an original, if a copy is different then we conclude someone either made an intentional change or an error. This print-centric mindset values identical copies and devalues variation—and distorts how we experience the Bible.

The variations between these proverbs are best explained by multiple face-to-face performances. Performances by parents to children, teachers to students, and storytellers to audiences repeated over and over again resulted in parallel versions. In a primarily face-to-face media culture, there is not one "original" but, instead, evidence of many performances trying to communicate the same points (or have similar effects). When scribes went to write these traditions to support ongoing education-enculturation, one wrote one version from their memory while another scribe wrote a slightly different version.[30] When a scribe knew two versions, sometimes they included them both.[31]

This process of memorization (or, better, internalization), re-performance, and then writing a version that may harmonize memories of many performances (or even writing multiple versions on different occasions) explains some variations in the Bible that were once thought to be copying changes or errors. In the early twentieth century two professors of comparative literature, Milman Parry and his student Albert Lord, studied Bosnian folk storytellers and observed that their use of stock formulas, scenes, and types was similar to the construction of Homer's *Iliad* and *Odyssey*. These storytellers believed

30. Ibid., 408–13, suggests that an Egyptian scribe familiar with Egyptian wisdom instruction (Amenemope) helped shape Israel's wisdom instruction, now reflected in Proverbs. He argues (413–15) that the Deuternomistic History (Deuteronomy—2 Kings), Isaiah, and Jeremiah (to name a few) show influence of writing-supported education using wisdom materials, some of which are collected in Proverbs. For more on this "multiformity" of tradition, see Raymond F. Person, *The Deuteronomic History and the Book of Chronicles: Scribal Works in an Oral World* (Atlanta: SBL Press, 2010).

31. An example of a scribe showing combined traditions is John 1:34. One manuscript tradition reads "elect one of God" and another reads "the Son of God"; some Latin manuscripts combine them to read "the elect son of God." Bruce Metzger and the United Bible Societies committee conclude that "the Son of God" is original, but this ignores the performances of which the manuscripts are evidence. "Elect one of God" was performed for some audiences and other audiences heard a combined "elect Son of God" when their copy of John was read. For those communities, that was the "original." Bruce M. Metzger, *A Textual Commentary on the Greek New Testament*, 2d ed. (Stuttgart: United Bible Societies, 1994), 172.

they were telling exactly the same story each time, but when word-for-word comparisons were made, it showed variations between each performance. When a different storyteller told a story, it further showed the marks of memorization and re-performance: the new storyteller abbreviated, replaced less-familiar terms with more-familiar ones, and explained parts of the story that the performer thought might be unfamiliar to the audience.[32]

In a communal setting, when the performer and the audience know the usual way a tradition is performed, the audience may object if it varies from the expected form.[33] The audience is not always interested in word-for-word accuracy but the consistency of meaning or, better, *effect* on the audience (recall the discussion about communication's effect vs. effort required by the audience). Performers and audiences mutually reinforce specific ways to perform a saying, story, or message. This encourages conservatism and limits innovation. Paradoxically, this also encourages a performer to vary words, to abbreviate, or even to expand on the tradition in order to increase the impact on an audience.

Writing memories makes it possible to separate the text from the face-to-face experience of a performer and an audience. Perhaps because royal administrations seem to be the first to use writing, in ancient media cultures writing has an effect of transmitting authority and power across distances. The Persian king gave Ezra a letter that authorized him wherever he went to collect and safely transport silver and gold—and to teach the "laws of God" and punish those who do not obey (Ezra 7:11–28). Scribes were given authority to handle texts, in other words, power is yielded to them. Scribes were called upon to re-perform the material, that is, to repeat it aloud to audiences (even other scribes who reinscribe the words) and to interpret it for new situations. These scribal performances maintained and extended its impact on new audiences. When Ezra performed the king's letter before an audience, it represented and enacted the king's will at a

32. Carr, *Formation of the Hebrew Bible*, 14.

33. Or, the audience may be challenged or amused by a significant departure from a fixed form, for example, how a spoof re-performs a beloved work.

distance. For later performances of the book of Ezra in other places and times, the king's letter evoked praise of God: "Blessed be the Lord, the God of our ancestors . . ." (Ezra 7:27).

It is perhaps not surprising that writing associated with God is associated with heavenly administration and written memories of experiences with God are given extraordinary authority. Not only with Persian authorization, Ezra teaches and enforces God's instruction, the Torah.

The scribal transmission of biblical traditions reveals a balance of preservation and revision. Carr writes:

> On the one hand, the oral-written tradition (as a whole, not its individual compositional parts) was regarded as a holy, precious set of messages from an otherwise inaccessible past, to be preserved and passed on to future generations. One's virtuosity as a student and scholar was proven by one's ability to cite and reproduce portions of the tradition, generally from memory. On the other hand, documented cases of transmission history show that ancient scholars did revise such traditions in multiple ways, generally expanding the tradition, but sometimes omitting parts, inserting additional traditions deemed relevant, and/or harmonizing/coordinating one part of the tradition with another.[34]

The scribe is both empowered to maintain traditions and to coordinate the overall traditions and their impact on contemporary audiences.

The role of memory also changed with increased use of writing. Performances could be compared with both written texts and memory. Whether Ezra or Jesus could read fluently is beside the point: when Nehemiah 8 and Luke 4 picture them standing to read from a scroll, it portrays them in a performance that is memory-based and writing-assisted. An audience would assume as they heard Nehemiah or Luke that it was not Ezra or Jesus' first time "reading" it aloud—they would know that recitation of passages was an important part of the educational process.[35] A reader knew what the text says well enough they only need to glance at it to trigger the memories of what to say

34. Carr, *Formation of the Hebrew Bible*, 100.

35. See Dan Nässelqvist, *Public Reading in Early Christianity: Lectors, Manuscripts, and Sound in the Oral Delivery of John 1–4* (Leiden: Brill, 2015), 27–29.

next. As Dan Nässelqvist writes about early Christian readers, "The lector analyzed the text beforehand in order to interpret—and decide upon—its division, prosody, delivery, and so on."[36] More than the text itself, the reader must have built skills and experience for clear and fluent pronunciation and intonation that will have an effect on an audience. Recall the memory-fueled communication process discussed earlier: even today, when we read something, we see a familiar word, even a few letters, and naturally begin to anticipate what is coming next by drawing on our memories. You might have skipped reading this whole paragraph because you already guessed what my point was!

This process of memorization, performance, writing, re-performance, memorization, rewriting was ongoing throughout the formation of the Hebrew Bible and arguably at least the Gospels in the New Testament. There is widespread agreement among scholars that the traditions represented in the Bible were largely read aloud in communal settings. There is agreement that only a minority could pick up a scroll and codex and read it fluently (although there is disagreement about what percentage). There is disagreement about the role of a manuscript and to what extent these readings were memorized word for word or read with emotion, gestures, movement, or tonal variations. Some scholars, such as Larry Hurtado, Rafael Rodriguez, Dan Nässelqvist, and Chris Keith, argue that most readings would not be memorized or presented with features that may be understood as "dramatic."[37] Others, such as David Rhoads, Tom

36. Ibid., 27.

37. Larry W. Hurtado, "Oral Fixation and New Testament Studies?: 'Orality', 'Performance' and Reading Texts in Early Christianity" *New Testament Studies* 60, no. 3 (July 2014): 321–40. Rafael Rodríguez, *Oral Tradition and the New Testament: A Guide for the Perplexed* (London: Bloomsbury/T&T Clark, 2014); Nässelqvist, *Public Reading*. Chris Keith writes, "I don't think that anyone involved would deny that there is a 'performance' element to the reading of texts in early Christianity, by which I mean a reciprocal relationship between the reader and the audience. I, at least, would certainly not deny that. That's not the problem at all. The problem is with the further assertions that these events did not, or at least did not typically, involve the actual consultation of a manuscript; that is, that the readers didn't actually read (and, related, that scribes did not typically write, but rather composed orally). This is where I think there simply is not evidence enough to say this, and there is evidence quite to the contrary in Jewish, Greco-Roman, and early Christian sources. There's no doubt that orality was a very important factor in the ancient media environment. But it was not the only factor. And for me, the significant issue with orality is not that it made textuality unnecessary or irrelevant, but that it provided a context in which textuality functioned in diverse ways." Keith, "Hurtado on Oral Fixation in New Testament

Boomershine, Whitney Shiner, and Joanna Dewey, suggest that memorization was more commonplace and that emotion, gestures, tonal variation, and movement were an essential part of effective presentations.[38] I suggest that these factors are dependent upon the goals of the performer and expectations of the audience. An effective reader will have internalized the text through study and repetition, but the degree of memorization would vary. A "public reading" may be less emotional or have fewer gestures than a "recitation," but both are performances. A public reader or lector holding a manuscript in one or both hands will still have needed to study the text ahead of time to achieve adequate fluency. When reading the text, the reader will embody the text by unconsciously raising and lowering tone, moving eyes from text to audience, even gesturing with hands.

What matters is that we need to become aware of our media culture and our unconscious assumptions that shape how we experience biblical texts. Then, by illuminating our assumptions, we can better develop descriptions of ancient performance scenarios and how these biblical passages may be used in those scenarios.

For example, we can make some broad generalizations about people in the United States in the twenty-first century.[39] Our media culture is different from media cultures in biblical times:[40]

- Our education is less dependent on memory. We assume information can be easily accessed through the Internet or written materials.
- We assume there is a written original, and value it over copies that may be "corrupt."

Studies," http://historicaljesusresearch.blogspot.com/2014/06/hurtado-on-oral-fixation-in-new.html.

38. Rhoads, "Performance Criticism—Part I"; Boomershine, *Messiah of Peace*, 4; Whitney Shiner, *Proclaiming the Gospel: First-Century Performance of Mark* (Harrisburg, PA: Trinity Press International, 2003); Joanna Dewey, "Textuality in an Oral Culture: A Survey of the Pauline Traditions," in *Semeia 65: Orality and Textuality in Early Christian Literature*, ed. Joanna Dewey (Atlanta: Scholars Press, 1995), 37–65.
39. For example, see Bruce J. Malina, *The New Testament World: Insights from Cultural Anthropology*, 3d ed. (Louisville: Westminster John Knox, 2001), 76–78, for comparisons between Mediterranean and U.S. preferences (perhaps overdrawn).
40. See Loubser, *Oral and Manuscript Culture*, 17; and Robert M. Fowler, "Why Everything We Know about the Bible Is Wrong: Lessons from the Media History of the Bible," in Hearon and Ruge-Jones, eds., *Bible in Ancient and Modern Media*, 3–18.

- We measure "faithfulness" by word-for-word transmission.
- We expect an explicit comment when something has been altered, who altered it, and why.
- We assume access to and durability of written material.
- We separate "facts" from "interpretation."

In biblical times, we can generalize:

- Education was dependent on performance and memorization, with writing as support when available.
- Accessibility to multiple face-to-face performances made written originals less valuable.
- "Faithfulness" was measured by consistency of effects between performances.
- Words were changed without comment when appropriate for effect; summarization and expansion depending on the audience and situation.
- Written material could be rare and costly and was expected to decay.
- Written and face-to-face presentation of traditions were assumed to be the performer's interpretation.

Inquiry: World of the Text

Performance creates an alternative world with its own *actors, time, space, point of view,* and *standards of judgment*.[41] Narrative critics call the people in the story "characters," but performance critics usually call them "actors." For example, there are three actors in Luke 4:16–30: Jesus, the attendant who handles the scroll, and "all in the synagogue"—a group that can be analyzed as a single character.

41. See David Rhoads, Donald Mitchie, and Joanna Dewey, *Mark as Story: An Introduction to the Narrative of a Gospel*, 3d ed. (Minneapolis: Fortress Press, 2012); this third edition gives special attention to performance criticism. Ward and Trobisch, *Bringing the Word to Life*, 76–79, emphasize perspective (what I am calling "point of view"), setting, characters, and conflict.

Inside the world of Luke 4:16–30, the *time* is the Sabbath day, with two periods emphasized. First, the brief time required to read from the scroll of Isaiah is emphasized. Then, time is accelerated as Jesus' interpretation is summarized with the words "Today this scripture has been fulfilled in your hearing." The second emphasis is on Jesus' reaction to their amazement. Time slows down with Jesus' direct speech, the audience's response of rage, and the attempt to throw him off a cliff. A performer of Luke 4:16–30 will have to decide how best to convey the summarization of Jesus' speech to an audience so that they might understand the violent response of "all in the synagogue."

The *space* is defined by the synagogue inside the village and the cliff outside the village. Few other details are given about the space, including whether or not the synagogue was a building or only an open-air meeting place. Within Jesus' speech, space is further distinguished between Nazareth and Capernaum, Israel and Gentile territories such as Sidon, Zarephath, and Syria. A performance of this passage will create the impression of one space inside the synagogue and another outside the town at the cliff. Furthermore, the performer will create the effect of jealousy that another place such as Capernaum, Zarephath, or Syria might receive Jesus' favor rather than his hometown.

The world in Luke 4:16–30 is always shown through Jesus' *point of view*, although external to Jesus. If the text was made into a movie, the camera would be over Jesus' shoulder or on Jesus' face. We are not given information about what Jesus is thinking or internal emotions; the view is always external. When "all in the synagogue" respond in rage, it is an emotion that is evident to anyone who is paying attention, not a look inside their minds.

"Standards of judgment" is another term from narrative criticism. It refers to the values the text expresses. Jesus is valued as the one who fulfills Isaiah's prophecy. Luke's story emphasizes this point by slowing to show Jesus identify himself with Elijah and Elisha, prophets of old, who were rejected in Israel and brought healing to Gentiles. In this way, Luke's story also values those who receive Jesus' message without witnessing deeds of power. It further values those outside the community who receive Jesus, and devalues those inside who would reject Jesus and attempt to kill him.

One of the differences between narrative criticism and performance criticism is that the performer may respond in various ways to the standards of judgment presented by a text. A performer may choose to accentuate, minimize, or even resist these standards. A performer of Luke 4:16–30 can help an audience identify with those in the synagogue who are hurt and scandalized by Jesus' rejection by preparatory remarks and use of tone and gestures. Or, a performer may minimize any sympathy to identify instead with Jesus and his disciples who faced rejection and threats. Or, a performer can resist this standard by portraying Jesus as rude and assuming too much of his former neighbors. Inquiry into the world of the text reveals possible positions for a performer and audience to respond to the text.

Inquiry: World in Front of the Text

There is also a world in front of the text that shapes how we hear it. Every telling of a story is a new performance event, even if the same words are spoken by the same person in front of the same audience, because the situation will be different, even if slightly. With a different performer or audience, the same words of the text will be embodied and received in divergent ways. The new performance event opens a new world for the audience. Inquiry into the world in front of the text explores the ways a text was performed in the past and how it may be performed for the performance critic's audiences, including cues for gesture, tone, movement, emotion, and coherence.

For example, in what kind of scenarios was Luke 4 performed? Inquiry seeks evidence to describe how the Gospels in general were performed for early Christians and a more specific investigation could ask how Luke 4 was used, for example, by the church fathers.[42]

42. For much greater detail on the role of the lector or "public reader," see Nässelqvist, *Public Reading*; and William David Shiell, *Reading Acts: The Lector and the Early Christian Audience* (Boston: Brill, 2004).

Generally, Mark's Gospel seems to assume an informal setting that includes a give and take between audience and performer. He assumes that a public reader will explain the "desolating sacrilege" (13:14): "But when you see the desolating sacrilege set up where it ought not to be (let the reader understand), then those in Judea must flee to the mountains." The reference to a "desolating sacrilege" may not be clear to all hearers, and so the reader is cued to explain. This suggests a small, informal setting for the performance of Mark's Gospel.[43]

A more formal occasion seems to be suggested by Justin Martyr's *First Apology* (c. 150 CE), a scene described in chapter 1. In this case, the situation is a time of readings, interpretation, prayer, and celebration of the Eucharist. The readings from the "memoirs of the apostles" may have been quite long. Justin comments they would read "as long as time permits." The text is likely in the hand of the reader, although a fluent reader would have prepared ahead of time. He does not suggest that the person reading has any fixed role in the community, but reading a scroll or codex fluently would mark this person as possessing a unique skill. Justin implies that this is the regular pattern for Christians gathering on a Sunday.[44]

Other situations would include a reader (or "lector") as a formal role in a Christian community. The author of *2 Clement* (early second century CE) describes the reader as an increasingly formal role in Christian communities.[45] By the time of Cyprian (about 250 CE), the reader has a formal position in the community hierarchy, below presbyter and deacon.[46] Commodianus (third century) emphasized that a reader's lifestyle outside of worship affects how people receive their performances: "I warn certain readers only to consider, and to give material to others by an example of life, to avoid strife, and to shun so many quarrels; to repress terror, and never to be proud; moreover,

43. Nässelqvist, *Public Reading*, 15, refers to this kind of setting as "reading aloud in a small, controlled context, namely in a semi-private setting (for example, an author or lector who reads aloud at a literary gathering)."
44. This may be comparable to what Nässelqvist calls "reading aloud in a limited, but less controlled context, namely in a semi-private setting (for example, a lector who reads aloud at a dinner party)" (ibid.).
45. *2 Clement* 19:1.
46. Cyprian, *Epistle* 23; see *Apostolic Constitutions* 2.4.25; 3.1.11.

denounce the [so-called] 'righteous obedience' of wicked men. Make yourselves like to Christ your Master, O little ones."[47] The scenario is highly formal: a lector who has received training in reading clearly and loudly, whose lifestyle has been examined, and who has received ritual initiation into the role for the community. The codex may have been ritually carried to the place of reading and opened by an assistant for the lector to read. When the lector reads, the community gathered knows the person is trained and the act of reading itself is ritualized. At the same time, the community yields increased power to the lector.

To what extent did a reader use gestures, changes in tone, pitch, or speed, or movement to communicate? Physically holding a codex or manuscript limited one hand's movements. Culturally, as the lector's role became more formal and ritualized, they may have felt limited by fears that their reading would be overly emotional or compared to drama. The Christian writer Tatian (second century CE) expresses this concern, "I [do not] desire to be affected in sympathy with a man when he is winking and gesticulating in an unnatural manner. What wonderful or extraordinary thing is performed among you? They utter ribaldry in affected tones, and go through indecent movements."[48] For Tatian and his audiences, a performance would be less emotional and have fewer gestures and changes in tone.

In the various roles of lector in early Christianity, we can see the variety of performance scenarios for a passage such as Luke 4:16–30. Scenarios vary from informal to formal, from low ritualization to high ritualization, from high interaction between performer and audience during the performance to little or no interaction, from the performer as storyteller to the performer as trained and community-authorized lector.

Inquiry: Performance Possibilities

Inquiry leads us to examine a text carefully for performance cues: words, phrases that suggest culturally appropriate gestures and

47. Commodianus, *On Christian Discipline* 67.
48. Tatian, *Address to the Greeks* 22.

movement, emotions, and coherence. This is not to say that every performance will use these, but that the text itself suggests the possibilities for a performer to use them if appropriate for the specific audience and situation.

Gestures and Movement

Gestures are shaped by the realities of the human body that are the same now as in ancient times (two arms, legs, hands, etc.). Words for body parts cue the performer to gesture. For example, the English phrases, "on one hand" and "on the other hand," are descriptions of gestures, and corresponding terms exist in ancient Greek. Take the Sermon on the Mount (scene 6 from chapter 1) as an example. When Jesus says in the Sermon on the Mount, "Do not let your left hand know what your right hand is doing" (Matt 6:3), the performer may naturally hold their left hand out and then their right hand to illustrate.

Pronouns addressing the audience may cue gestures. In the Sermon on the Mount the switch from the general statements, "Blessed are . . ." to "Blessed are *you* . . . ," may suggest a gesture to the audience to emphasize this change. After describing a parent's response to children's needs, Jesus turns to the audience, "If *you* then . . ." (7:11).

Pronouns such as "this" or "that" can suggest pointing or gesturing at either a real or imaginary object. For example, when Jesus says, "In everything do to others as you would have them do to you; for *this* is the law and the prophets," the pronoun "this" may suggest a gesture to emphasize the equivalence with the law and prophets (7:12).

Sometimes gestures or movement may be suggested by cues that compare characters in a story or distinguish the audience from characters. When Jesus compares good trees and bad trees (7:15–19) or hearers and doers (7:24–27), this naturally suggests gestures comparing one kind of person to another. Gestures also respond to cues in the text that disassociate the audience from a group or characteristic. Jesus warns that "not everyone who says to me, 'Lord, Lord,' will enter the kingdom of heaven, but only the one who does the will of my Father in heaven" (7:21–23). A gesture away from the audience for "not everyone" helps the audience disassociate from a group mentioned.

Gestures may be cued by spatial references, such as "up," "down," "left," "right." Jesus says, "Every tree that does not bear good fruit is cut *down* and thrown into the fire" (7:19); "The rain *fell*, and the floods came, and the winds blew and beat against that house, and it *fell*—and great was its *fall*!" (7:27). It is natural to use the hands to aid the audience in visualizing these sentences and seeing the repetition and emphasis.

Although bodies are the same now as they were in ancient times, gestures are shaped by culture. What worked then may not work today, but we need to inquire into the role of gestures in performing a text then and now. William Sheill has done a service in describing gestures that ancient speakers recommended and the words that may have served as cues in the past.[49] Further work on ancient gestures will help us translate not only the words on the page but find appropriate gestures that communicate in modern cultures.

Embodying Emotions

The performer's emotional tone may be suggested by direct words such as *anger*, *grief*, *weeping*, and so on. When Jesus saw Mary weeping and those around her weeping, he also wept (John 11:33–34). The shortest verse in the Bible, "Jesus wept," was perhaps made the shortest since the storyteller paused and allowed the emotion its fullest bloom and impact. We shouldn't assume that the performer always imitates the word—the performer doesn't summon up tears—but in some way captures the emotional tone, in this case, grief and sadness.

Emotional tone is not simply a feature of the voice but the whole body. The position of the eyes, facial expressions, position of the shoulders may all be suggested by cues in the text. Psalm 123 suggests the tone of pleading with eyes lifted up, "To you I lift up my eyes, O you who are enthroned in the heavens!" Psalm 39:13 suggests that the

49. Shiell, *Reading Acts*.

performer perhaps bend away from God's silent gaze, "Turn your gaze away from me, that I may smile again, before I depart and am no more."

Other emotions may be more subtly indicated. For example, the emotion of frustration may be suggested by dialogue. When Jesus is trying to warn the disciples about the Pharisees and Herod, they misunderstand and Jesus responds with six questions beginning with, "Why are you talking about having no bread? Do you still not perceive or understand? Are your hearts hardened? Do you have eyes, and fail to see? Do you have ears, and fail to hear? And do you not remember?" (Mark 8:17–18). Mark piles on cues of frustration: rapid questions and accusations of hard hearts, blind eyes, deaf ears, and poor memories. These together suggest the performer may express frustration in tone of voice, facial expressions, and appropriate gestures.

Of course, in some instances the signals from the text are ambiguous and our inquiry discerns options. What is Jesus' emotional tone in the Garden of Gethsemane when he says, "Simon, are you asleep? Could you not keep awake one hour?" (Mark 14:37)? Is this frustration? It is certainly consistent with other episodes in Mark such as the one in the boat described above. Is this disappointment in a favored disciple? That may be indicated if one takes Jesus' use of "Simon" rather than "Peter" as a sign of Jesus' affection for Peter. Is this anger? "Simon," in this instance, is a repudiation of the nickname Jesus gave him. In this case, it is a sign of forgiveness when the messenger at the empty tomb calls him "Peter" once again (Mark 16:7).

In general, every text and passage has an emotional tone just as every audience will have a prior emotional state that will be affected by the performance. The performance critic reads the text closely for cues and guides to the emotional tone of the passage. In the stage of imagination, each should be tried to see if it creates a coherent whole in performance.

Coherence

Performance both reveals problems in the coherence of a text and also illuminates clues in the text that suggest how it all hangs together.

By "coherence," we mean how a text fits together, that it becomes a seamless whole for an audience. As I will discuss in chapter 5, one of the payoffs for performance criticism is that it reunites a text that is often dissolved in the critical gaze of scholarship.

For example, Philip Ruge-Jones observes that when one reads Mark's Gospel silently, it feels fragmented.[50] Scholars have long thought that the fragmentary nature of Mark's Gospel is one of the reasons that Matthew and Luke wrote their Gospels. The fourth-century historian and church leader Eusebius of Caesarea quotes John the Elder to say that Mark didn't write in order, but wrote "down single points as he remembered them."[51] In other words, Mark has long been experienced as disorderly.

When the Gospel of Mark is performed, the audience feels it is whole. After hearing Mark performed as a whole, Donald Juel wrote,

> The person who "performed" Mark . . . recited it in such a way that the breaks in the story were not a problem. The sense of coherence was accomplished in several ways, like changing positions and looking at different sections of the audience. It worked. The audience had little sense that the Gospel was deficient as a narrative. There were gaps and jumps, but the way they were handled by the performer made them enticing rather than irritating and distracting.[52]

Preparing to perform Mark's Gospel reveals the problem of coherence. Cues within the text itself suggest how to perform it coherently, which is how Juel experienced it.

Inquiry examines the text closely for clues to coherence. The oldest manuscripts of Mark's Gospel suggest that the story ended with the cliff-hanging flight of the women from the empty tomb: "So they went out and fled from the tomb, for terror and amazement had seized them; and they said nothing to anyone, for they were afraid" (Mark 16:8). How is this a coherent ending to the story? The evidence of

50. Philip Ruge-Jones, "The Word Heard: How Hearing a Text Differs from Reading One," in Hearon and Ruge-Jones, eds., *Bible in Ancient and Modern Media*, 101–13.
51. Eusebius, *Ecclesiastical History* 3.39.15.
52. Donald Juel, "The Strange Silence of the Bible," *Interpretation* 51 (1997): 8, quoted in Ruge-Jones, "The Word Heard," 111.

manuscripts with alternative endings suggests that other readers and performers found it unsatisfying.

Scholars who have read the text closely have detected clues in this ending that suggest coherence, and also suggest the ending is suited to performance (see scene 8 in chapter 1). Two intertwined issues that run throughout Mark's Gospel are (1) who will tell the story about Jesus and (2) the obedience of the disciples to Jesus' instructions, especially under pressure. Usually, it is not the disciples who are telling the story. Ironically, they are often the least obedient. Jesus tries to get people he healed not to spread the news, but they often do anyway. When Jesus healed a leper at the beginning of the story, Jesus instructed him not to tell anyone—but the man went out anyway and told others what happened and spread the word (Mark 1:44–45). When Jesus healed people with unclean spirits, he ordered them not to reveal his identity (Mark 3:11–12). He told Jairus's family not to talk about his daughter's resuscitation (5:43). We could continue to list examples. Scholars have referred to this as the "messianic secret" theme in Mark: Jesus does not want people to tell the story until after the resurrection. He explicitly says this to the disciples after Peter, James, and John have a vision of him transfigured with Moses and Elijah: "As they were coming down the mountain, he ordered them to tell no one about what they had seen, until after the Son of Man had risen from the dead" (9:9). The time for telling the story is after the resurrection.

The abrupt ending to Mark's Gospel is coherent when tied to the theme of the disciples' failure to understand and follow directions. By ending abruptly with the women running from the tomb, telling no one, the question is implicitly posed to the audience of Mark's Gospel: "Will you tell the story? Will you tell all you have heard even when you are terrified and afraid in front of trials and powers that may threaten you?" (Mark 13:9–11; see Mark's emphasis on "for the sake of the gospel" in 8:35). The text itself gives clues for the coherence of its abrupt ending. This coherence is apparent with close study of the themes of the text and its early performance situations.

Inquiry: Discerning Potential Effects of Performance

After describing a performance scenario based on details of the text, the dynamics of media cultures, and relevant information from archaeology and other disciplines, we can begin to discern what the potential effects of performance may be.

For example, we have evidence in manuscripts that the scenario of performing the end of Mark's Gospel seemed incomplete to some hearers. After hearing the story end with the women fleeing the tomb, some thought it needed a more satisfying ending for their audiences. As a result, we have at least four different performance scenarios indicated by the four manuscript traditions. The first tradition is the ending at verse 8. This ending seems to have the effect of calling the audience to do better than the women and the disciples who have not told the story in the face of fear, especially fear of persecution. It may have the further effect of encouraging disciples who feel they have failed Jesus (like Peter and the women) that they have another opportunity for faithfulness.

The second "shorter ending" suggests an audience that esteemed Peter. By using this ending, the performer asserts that Mark's Gospel is sacred, imperishable, and that the audience receives "eternal salvation" through its proclamation: "And all that had been commanded them they told briefly to those around Peter. And afterward Jesus himself sent out through them, from east to west, the sacred and imperishable proclamation of eternal salvation."

In another version (usually called "the longer ending," vv. 9–20), performers summarized resurrection appearances that are described in other Gospels, suggesting an audience that was aware of these other stories and expected them. The performer who uses this ending portrays the women as finally telling the story: "Now after he rose early on the first day of the week, he appeared first to Mary Magdalene, from whom he had cast out seven demons. She went out and told those who had been with him, while they were mourning and weeping. But when they heard that he was alive and had been seen by her, they would not believe it" (Mark 16:9–11). In both the shorter and longer endings, the performers are clear on their perspective: the women did tell the story, revising the judgment in verse 8 that the women fled from the tomb and said nothing to anyone. But a new problem has emerged in this third tradition: the women were not believed. The longer ending goes on to show Jesus appearing to the disciples to chastise them for not believing and encourage them to go out and tell the story.

A fourth tradition tries to explain why the disciples and others did not believe. The disciples excused themselves, explaining that the age is under Satan and that is why people are not believing their testimony. This performance suggests an audience that is frustrated in telling the story, not because of persecution, but lack of response. The performer, by including this ending, offers an explanation and encouragement to tell the story even as "other terrible things draw near."

Elisabeth Schüssler-Fiorenza, Birger Gerhardsson, and others have taken the focus on the women to indicate an early performance scenario in which the women have gathered men and women to hear their story.[53] Antoinette Wire and Joanna Dewey suggest that it was the women who initially were telling the whole story of Jesus as a way to explain the significance of the resurrection and in obedience to the messenger's instructions.[54] We can take the women gathered down by the river in Philippi as an example of gatherings where women told stories and prayed (scene 9 from chapter 1, from Acts 16:11–15). Chloe would be an example of a woman who brought stories of Christians in Corinth to Paul (1 Cor 1:11). Phoebe likely delivered and read Paul's letter to the Roman Christians (Rom 16:1).

53. Elisabeth Schüssler-Fiorenza, *In Memory of Her* (New York: Crossroad, 1983), 332; Birger Gerhardsson, "Mark and the Female Witnesses," in *Dumu-E2-Dub-Ba-A: Studies in Honor of Ake W. Sjoberg*, ed. H. Behrens, D. Loding, and M. T. Roth (Philadelphia: University of Pennsylvania Museum, 1989), 218–23; Samuel Byrskog, *Story as History—History as Story* (Tübingen: Mohr Siebeck, 2000), 75–78. See also Holly E. Hearon, *The Mary Magdalene Tradition: Witness and Counter-Witness in Early Christian Communities* (Collegeville, MN: Michael Glazier, 2004); Joanna Dewey, "From Storytelling to Written Text: The Loss of Early Christian Women's Voices," *Biblical Theology Bulletin* 26, no. 2 (1996): 71–78.

54. Antoinette Clark Wire, *The Case for Mark Composed in Performance* (Eugene, OR: Cascade, 2011), 183–86; Joanna Dewey, "Women on the Way: A Reconstruction of Late First-Century Women's Storytelling," in Hearon and Ruge-Jones, eds., *Bible in Ancient and Modern Media*, 36–48.

In the same way, the prominence of Mary Magdalene in the four Gospels suggests she was a primary early teller of the story of Jesus' resurrection.[55] Later performers invoke her name as they tell the story as a kind of citation, making it clear that their story is dependent on her story. In chapter 1, we reconstructed this scenario into scene 8:

Scene 8: *A group of women have gathered in the home of Mary from Magdala. They have heard she and a few other women were the first ones at the tomb of Jesus, and that Mary saw messengers that must have been from heaven. They told her that Jesus was alive! As she has done for weeks, she insists on telling the story from the beginning, to build up to the dramatic experience she had at the tomb and encourage her audience to tell the story to others. "This is the beginning of the Good News of Jesus Christ, the Son of God. As it is written in the prophet Isaiah, 'See, I am sending my messenger ahead of you. . . .'"*

As later performers change the ending to fit their preferences and the expectations of their audience, the effects of the ending change. The original, abrupt ending of Mark's Gospel may have moved audiences to become storytellers even in the face of persecution. The shorter ending satisfies the expectation that the story has been told, and focuses the audience instead on its sacred quality and purpose to proclaim eternal salvation. The longer ending recalls the audience's memory of resurrection appearances heard in other Gospels. The longest ending tries to explain why audiences do not believe the story and encourages the audience to persist in telling it.

Up to this point, inquiry has focused on the text itself and how the text was used. Because the goal is a re-performance of the text in our time and place, the task of inquiry also must include analysis of the contemporary audience and situation.

55. Richard Bauckham, *Jesus and the Eyewitnesses: The Gospels as Eyewitness Testimony* (Grand Rapids: Eerdmans, 2006), 48–51. Gerald O'Collins and Daniel Kendall, "Mary Magdalene as Major Witness to Jesus' Resurrection," *Theological Studies* 48 (1987): 631–46. Origen, in the third century, had to defend Celsus's charge that the resurrection was based on the witness of a "hysterical female" (*Contra Celsum* 2.55).

World in Front of the Text: Contemporary Audience and Situation

Human beings naturally select signs (words, gestures, facial expressions, pacing, movement, tone, volume) that they believe will lead their audience to the intended meaning. Usually this process is subconscious. A performer will "read" the audience for responses that indicate they are experiencing the desired effects, and adjust the performance until the performer receives the feedback they are looking for.

Many performers find it helpful to inquire into their audience before performing and to choose language and other signs that will have the desired impact. This kind of inquiry can change the very translation of the text, and so should be done in the preparation stage.

For example, a performer may investigate:[56]

Goals (or "effects") of the performance on the new audience. Based on the inquiry into the text and its effects in the past, what effects does the performer want the current audience to experience? For example, is a performance of Mark's Gospel intended to move the audience to retell the story (fitting the original ending)? To "proclaim eternal salvation" (with the shorter ending)? Or some other goals?

Other goals may arise from the situation of the new audience. This may require an analysis of the socioeconomic location of the audience, their emotional state, and what's going on in the world. Matthew, for example, seems to retell the story to encourage disciples to go beyond their comfortable community to tell the story of Jesus and show it in care of their unbelieving neighbors (Matt 28:19–20; see 25:34–40). How will the story be told in such a way to achieve those goals for the present audience?

The use of a physical text, gestures, tone variation, and movement should be determined by considering the effect on the audience. Some audiences will receive an overly dramatic performance as demeaning to the text or the ritual situation. Although a performer may have the text completely internalized, they may choose to hold a book and

56. For a more complete discussion of these issues, see Swanson, *Provoking the Gospel: Methods.*

appear to read from it in order to create the effect of reverence. In other cases, if the performer does not have a text in hand but performs entirely from memory, the audience may become so distracted by the performer's memorization skills that they fail to experience the performance. Other audiences may clap or laugh or talk to the performer during the performance. Inquiry should consider the effects of the performance for the specific audience.

Ethical issues in performance. Every performance is an intervention into culture, power relations, and identity. The performer should become aware of the ways a text has been used in the past to silence, exploit, or oppress people. For example, a performance of 1 Corinthians 7 has to consider that it contains passages that have been used to support slavery in the United States and also to persuade women to stay in abusive marriages. Will the audience be aware of the way the text has been used in unhealthy and destructive ways? Should the performer include a discussion of these issues before or after a performance?

One of the challenges when I perform the book of Revelation is the issue of violence against women, violence that appears to be sanctioned by God. For example, the glorified Jesus tells the congregation in Thyatira that a Christian prophetess will be "thrown on a bed" and "I will strike her children dead" (Rev 2:22–23). I explain that John is a man of his time, performing his vision in a graphic way to shock his audiences to change. I draw on the central ethics of "love your neighbor as yourself" and "love your enemies" to counter these passages. A performer cannot simply perform some texts without addressing that people may take it to sanction unhealthy values and power relations.

Language preferences of an audience. What idioms does this audience know? In many faith communities, a jargon may be assumed, for example, experiences attached to words like "faith," "grace," "love," and "righteousness." But if the audience will be composed of people from outside faith communities, these words will take too much processing effort and may fail to make an impact. The performer may have to retranslate words or rephrase passages shaped by the knowledge of the audience and the desired effect.

The space of the performance area. What is the appropriate range of volume for the space in order for people at the back to hear clearly? Is there reverberation in the room that requires slower speech? Is there room for movement? Are there areas where the line of sight for some of the audience may be blocked? How far must the performer turn her head or body in order to make eye contact with all members of the audience? How big will the gestures be in order to be seen at the back of the room? If the performance involves helping the audience imagine people or places, where in the space would it be best to focus these imaginary people or locations?

Translation for Performance

Although not all performance critics work with biblical languages, translation for performance integrates the insights gained in this process of preparation. The process of internalizing and performing a text will further change how a text is translated. In developing a translation, James Maxey suggests a paradigm of hospitality that values carefulness, authenticity, and transparency.[57] I will briefly describe these values here and give more detailed examples in the next two chapters.

Carefulness indicates that the translator handles the text with care as it is brought into a new situation for a new audience. A performance critic demonstrates care in the close examination of the text as described above. A careful translation is attentive to the details of the text and the effects they may have on various audiences, and attempts to create similar effects in contemporary audiences. For example, Paul's First Letter to the Thessalonians (scene 10 from chapter 1) explicitly indicates it was meant to be read aloud (1 Thess 5:27). The translator considers the sound of the words in Greek and the way they may indicate emphasis or please the ear. As Paul begins his

57. James Maxey, "Alternative Evaluative Concepts to the Trinity of Bible Translation," in *Translating Values*, ed. Piotr Blumczynski and John Gillespie (New York: Palgrave Macmillan, 2016), 57–80.

thanksgiving for the Thessalonian Christians in 1:2, he uses five words that begin with *p*- sounds, two of which involve the sound *pan*- (often translated "all"). The effect emphasizes the exuberance of Paul's gratitude and would be pleasing to the Greek ear. How can these subtle effects be brought into a new language?[58]

Authenticity refers to the attention the translator gives to her relationship to the audience and their language and preferred medium. The performance critic is not developing a translation in the abstract, but in a concrete relationship. If a relationship does not yet exist, the performance critic takes time in preparation to begin to build an authentic relationship. In the process of preparation, as the critic studies the audience she is listening for appropriate language and nonverbal cues to express the text in a way it may lead to appropriate effects. For example, translating the *pan*- words consistently with the English "all" (e.g., "all the time" and "all of you") may be an appropriate sound path in English for some audiences to follow. Authentic translations are the result of asking, "What is appropriate for this audience?," and listening carefully to the answers.

Transparency preserves the otherness of the Bible and the otherness of the host community. To create a transparent translation is to maintain an effect of strangeness. Biblical traditions can't be domesticated, power relations can't be fixed between performer and audience, and a text can't be made to affirm an audience entirely for who they are. For example, an English translation of 1 Thessalonians should make clear through some awkwardness that it applies to a community of Christians in another place and time.

Formatting for Performance

It is helpful to format the translation in a way that aids internalization, the next step in the process. Most Bibles are formatted in block paragraphs that do not assist the performer in seeing the phrasing

58. The work of Margaret Lee, Brandon Scott, Tom Boomershine, and Dan Nässelqvist on sound mapping suggests a beginning point for this work. See Margaret Ellen Lee and Bernard Brandon Scott, *Sound Mapping the New Testament* (Salem, OR: Polebridge, 2009).

or sense-units. I prefer to break the text up so that each line has only one verbal form and dependent clauses are indented below each line. I use footnotes to discuss translation issues and give references to commentaries. I use Microsoft Word's "Track Changes" feature to add performance suggestions, including intonation, gestures, facial expression, movement, and emotion (see appendices A and B, below, for examples). For further discussion about formatting for performances, see Ernst Wendland's *Orality and the Scriptures: Composition, Translation, and Transmission.*[59]

Step 2: Internalization

After preparing the passage for performance, the next step is to internalize the passage and its performance for a contemporary audience. We use the word *internalize* rather than the word *memorize* because an effective performance is not necessarily based on word-for-word memorization but, rather, on a presentation that maximizes desired effects for reasonable effort by the audience. "Internalization" implies that the text is understood deeply by the performer without referring directly to a physical text. A performer who has internalized a text can begin at any place within the story, vary language to fit an audience, summarize or expand depending on the constraints and possibilities of the performance situation.

As I will show in more detail in the next two chapters, there are many different ways to internalize a text. Most of them involve repeating a text over and over in various ways until it can be presented with minimal reference to a physical text. The "text" has become a part of the performer. When it is performed, the audience "reads" its embodiment by the performer.

Tom Boomershine, in *Story Journey: An Invitation to the Gospel as*

59. Ernst Wendland, *Orality and the Scriptures: Composition, Translation, and Transmission* (Dallas: SIL, 2013). See also Ernst R. Wendland and J. P. Louw, *Graphic Design and Bible Reading: Exploratory Studies in the Typographical Representation of the Text of Scripture in Translation* (Capetown: Bible Societies of South Africa, 1993). This way of formatting is based on the insights of discourse criticism. For a good introduction, see Steven E. Runge, *Discourse Grammar of the Greek New Testament: A Practical Introduction for Teaching and Exegesis* (Peabody, MA: Hendrickson, 2010).

Storytelling, suggests breaking the passage down into episodes or "chunks" that can be understood and remembered.[60] Boomershine emphasizes the communal aspect of storytelling, which others amplify.

Richard Swanson emphasizes internalizing a text with others in his book *Provoking the Gospel: Methods to Embody Biblical Storytelling through Drama*.[61] He suggests gathering a group who will read the story aloud together and discuss what they see, reading it over and over until it can be told without the paper in hand, moving spontaneously while trying different emotional tones.

Michael Williams, Dennis Smith, and other authors have published *The Storyteller's Companion to the Bible* in thirteen volumes. Each includes insights into how to internalize the story. They encourage using an introduction and comments during the performance to explain social and cultural motifs and Jewish traditions that modern audiences may not know. These comments are internalized during this step.[62]

In *Bringing the Word to Life: Engaging the New Testament through Performing It*, Richard Ward and David Trobisch also suggest internalizing a text by working with a group and repeated readings.[63] On each successive reading, the reader experiments with different intonations and pauses, then gestures, facial expressions, and movement. The group gives feedback on each experiment. Through repetition and experimentation, the text is gradually internalized.

Step 3: Performance

This is where it all comes together. The performer has internalized not only the text but what has been learned about the world behind the text, the world of the text, and the world in front of the text. The text, which has been broken down in many ways by analyzing it carefully, is reassembled into a seamless whole in the performance

60. Tom Boomershine, *Story Journey: An Invitation to the Gospel as Storytelling* (Nashville: Abingdon, 1988).
61. Swanson, *Provoking the Gospel: Methods to Embody Biblical Storytelling through Drama* (Cleveland: Pilgrim, 2004).
62. For example, Michael E. Williams and Dennis E. Smith, *The Storyteller's Companion to the Bible: Volume 11, Parables of Jesus* (Nashville: Abingdon, 2006).
63. Ward and Trobisch, *Bringing the Word to Life*, 69–71.

itself. Communication happens: a performer embodies a text for an audience in a given situation and all are transformed in some way by the experience.

One performance may simply be standing with a group of friends summarizing the story of early Christians at worship as shared by Justin (scene 11 in chapter 1). It is informal, hardly word for word, no text is present, but it is a performance nonetheless.

Another performance may be a reader standing in church or synagogue to read an assigned passage for the day. A text is present in a book—perhaps a lectionary or other ritually appropriate volume. The reader looks often at the book, reading even word for word. To do anything else would be to show disrespect for the reading and the audience's expectations. If the reader has practiced, internalizing the text ahead of time, the reading will include changes in inflection that help the audience understand the text and its effects. If the reader has not prepared, the audience will have to work harder, put in more effort to understand why and how this passage may be relevant to them. At bare minimum, a hearer may feel they have experienced worship because they heard a ritual reading of the text. This is often a desired effect of a reading! This performance is formal, highly ritualized, but a performance nonetheless.

Another performance may be a gathering where a performer shares a longer passage from the Bible, even a whole book to an audience gathered for that purpose only. In the next two chapters, I will describe how I prepared, internalized, and performed the books of Habakkuk and Revelation for various audiences and how we were changed through these experiences.

3

Performing Habakkuk

The basic method of performance criticism is *prepare, internalize,* and *perform*. These three steps roughly correlate to the three aspects of performance: *inquiry, imagination,* and *intervention.* As I demonstrate below, however, preparation requires not only inquiry but also imagination and intervention. Internalization is not only an act of imagination but also depends on inquiry and intervention. The performance itself integrates inquiry, imagination, and intervention into one experience for performer and audience.

I have chosen Habakkuk as the first example to illustrate the method and payoff of performance criticism. My translation and analysis is based on Jeanette Mathews's book, *Performing Habakkuk: Faithful Re-enactment in the Midst of Crisis,* although the translation has been modified by my process of preparing, internalizing, and performing the text.[1] (See appendix A for my translation and performance notes.) The first step of the method is *preparation,* which inquires into the text: the world behind the text, the world of the text, and the world in front of the text.

1. Jeanette Mathews, *Performing Habakkuk: Faithful Re-Enactment in the Midst of Crisis* (Eugene, OR: Wipf & Stock, 2012).

Inquiry: The World Behind the Text

By the "world behind the text," we mean the social situation, experience, and people of the first performances out of which the text emerged. In this case, it is a prophet called Habakkuk, the situation in Judah and the surrounding region, and the leaders, wealthy landowners, and peasants who may have heard Habakkuk. We look for hints in the text that correlate with archaeology, other writings, and cultural anthropology to understand what was going on that gave rise to the book we now call Habakkuk.

What little we know about the prophet Habakkuk comes from the text itself. The text portrays him as a prophet who experiences God taking responsibility for the "rise of the Chaldeans" (1:6). From commentaries, we discover that "Chaldean" is the name of one of the tribes that led the emergence of the Babylonian Empire.[2] Nabopolassar (d. 604 BCE) led his armies to a decisive victory over the waning Assyrian Empire and their Egyptian allies at Carchemish in 605 BCE. By referring to the "rise of the Chaldeans," the text suggests that Habakkuk was active during this period.

Two themes emerge from our inquiry into this time in Judah: the excesses of prosperity and increasing violence. Habakkuk lived in a time of prosperity. Before the rise of the Babylonians, the southern kingdom of Judah was relatively prosperous under the reign of Josiah (641–609 BCE). The northern kingdom (often referred to as "Israel") had been conquered by the Assyrians in 722 BCE, but a hundred years later the Assyrian Empire was in decline. This vacuum opened political and economic space for smaller countries like Judah to prosper and resist the usual imperial ambitions of Assyria and Egypt.

2. For example, see J. J. M. Roberts, *Nahum, Habakkuk, and Zephaniah*, The Old Testament Library (Louisville: Westminster John Knox, 1991), 82–83.

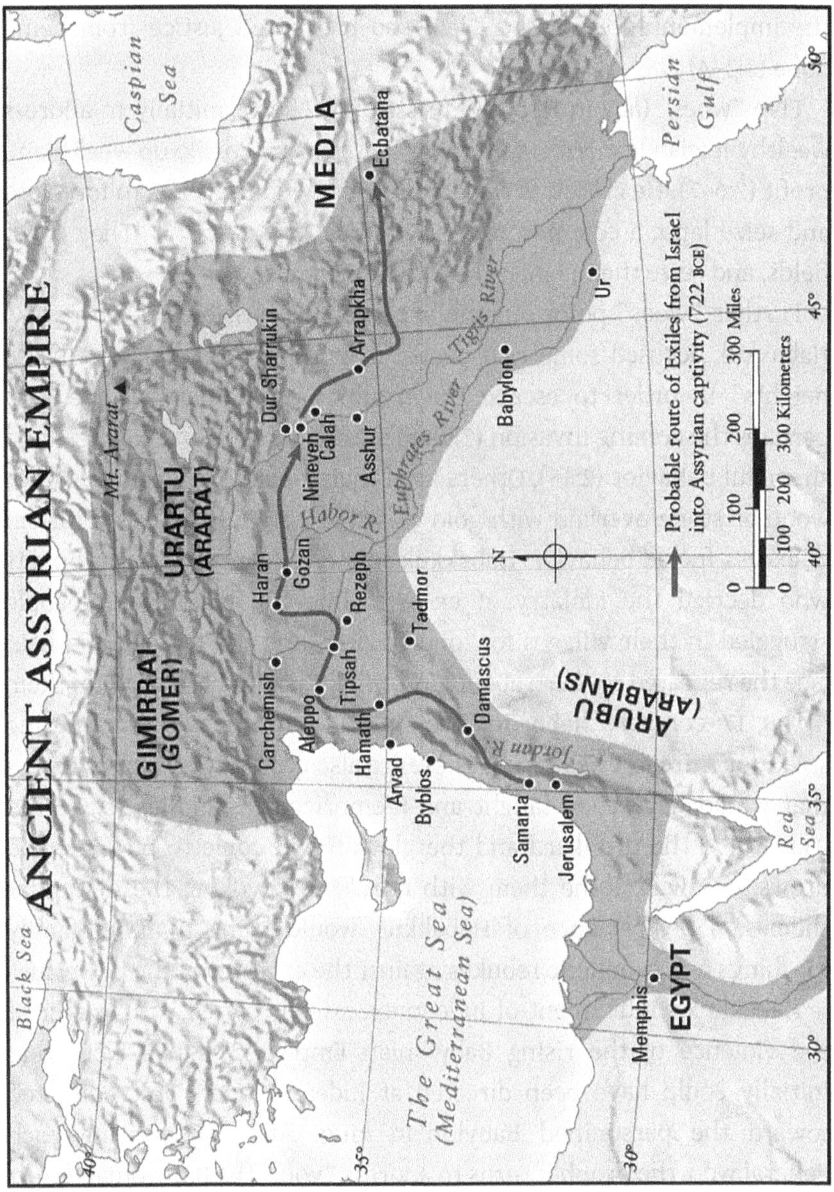

In this political and economic space, the rich could become richer. With too much power and wealth, it was easy for them to be excessive. Habakkuk sees wicked Judeans limiting the efforts of the righteous (1:4). Strife and contention, meaning turmoil in leadership, paralyzed the implementation of God's law and prevented justice from being done (1:3–4).

Five "woes" (*hoy* in Hebrew) in chapter 2 seem initially to address wealthy Jewish leaders. Habakkuk warns those who pile up wealth and profit (2:6–7). He criticizes rich landowners who use loans to foreclose and seize land, a common prophetic topic (e.g., Mic 2:2, "They covet fields, and seize them; houses, and take them away").

Further "woes" point out the excess made possible by prosperity. Habakkuk accused some rich people of building their homes "in the heights" in order to escape the troubles of ordinary people, and perhaps the coming invasion (2:9). Some encouraged drunkenness and shameful behavior (2:15). Others used their wealth to make idols from wood or stone overlaid with gold or silver (2:18–19). In this criticism of excess-fueled behavior, Habakkuk sounds like many other prophets who decried the idolatry of excess while the majority of people struggled in their villages for food, shelter, and fire to cook and heat (see the repeated concern about land, villages, and those living in them in 2:8, 17; compare "labor for fire" in 2:13 with the widow gathering sticks for a fire in 1 Kgs 17:10). These are also typical topics for proverbs that would have been taught and memorized in families (e.g., Prov 23:21, ". . . the drunkard and the glutton will come to poverty, and drowsiness will clothe them with rags."). By evoking these familiar themes, a performance of Habakkuk would bring to mind family teachings and prophetic rebukes against the excesses of the powerful.

Habakkuk's indictment of Judean excesses is paired with horror at the violence of the rising Babylonian Empire. The five woes that initially could have been directed at Judean leaders are redirected toward the personified Babylonian king. After announcing each general woe, the prophet turns to address "you," the Babylonian king.

With the rise of the Babylonians, violence throughout the region increased. King Josiah died in 609 BCE in a battle against the Egyptians at Megiddo (2 Kgs 23:29 // 2 Chron 35:20–27). Some scholars speculate that Josiah was trying to ally Judah with the strengthening Babylonian Empire. Habakkuk saw that God was behind the Babylonian's growing influence. Was Josiah's fatal battle against the Egyptians the result of proclamations by prophets like Habakkuk? It is difficult to say. Habakkuk's view of the Babylonian Empire is resoundingly negative. He expresses his dismay that God would choose such an evil, treacherous tool as the Babylonians, which may reflect feelings about Babylonian failure to protect Josiah and Judah from the Egyptians (1:12–17).

After Josiah's death, Judah became a vassal state of the Egyptians. The Pharaoh deposed Josiah's son Jehoahaz and put his older brother Jehoiakim on the throne (2 Kgs 23:31). The Egyptians demanded tribute of silver and gold. Egyptian control of Judah was short-lived: the Egyptians had to defend against a Babylonian invasion and to assist their Assyrian allies. After the Egyptian and Assyrian defeat at Carchemish in 605 BCE, the Babylonian rise was secure and further developed by Nabopolassar's son, Nebuchadnezzar II—who later would conquer Judah and destroy the Jerusalem temple in 587 BCE. Violence was on the rise and, from Habakkuk's perspective, Babylon was the cause.

The book of Habakkuk suggests a complex media culture. The text presents Habakkuk as a prophet who can write on tablets: "Write the vision and make it plain on the tablets" (2:2). This written vision (engraved in stone) was expected to be carried by a runner for others to read and announce throughout the land. This positioned Habakkuk among the small minority of scribally trained people who also had access to a network of runners who brought communication throughout Judah.

Habakkuk was also involved with a community that sings psalms (3:2–15). Even if we take the musical instructions as a later addition, they suggest early performances included singing.[3] This community had the leadership to teach the psalms and train musicians. Scholars debate whether or not this was a song used in the Jerusalem temple or in some group outside the temple, and also whether this was a

3. Theodore Hiebert, *God of My Victory: The Ancient Hymn in Habakkuk 3* (Atlanta: Scholars Press, 1986).

preexisting psalm that the author adapted or if the author composed the psalm himself.

From a performance-critical point of view, it is more important to see that early performances of Habakkuk included a transition from spoken to sung media for 3:2–15. The change is announced in 3:1, including the tune (which is now lost to us): "A prayer of Habakkuk the prophet, to the tune of Shigionoth." This change suggests that the performance of Habakkuk becomes a kind of worship experience, even if not used in a worship setting. Singing, in general, makes memorization easier because it engages a different part of the brain. Singing is often more emotional, which makes more of an impression upon hearers. Singing also fits the content of the book, the movement from the prophet's lament and announcement of woes to the response of trust in God's faithfulness.

Because of the psalm, the performance of chapter 3 becomes explicitly interactive with the audience. The psalm form suggests the audience may have sung together with the performer in a familiar way that the psalms were often used.[4] Initially, the audience may not have known the psalm, but in repeated performances the audience may have memorized the psalm and sung along at this point. We still don't know what the Hebrew word *selah* means, only that it is used frequently in the psalms and seems to suggest some kind of musical response. The use of *selah* in 3:3, 9, 13 may indicate a musical interlude or a refrain.

Finally, the presence of instruments is suggested by the final instruction, "To the director, to the tune of Niginoth" (3:19). The assumption is that there is a "director" who would lead instrumental music, perhaps both to accompany the psalm as well as to provide a time of reflection on Habakkuk's final words (3:16–19).

Inquiry: World of the Text

The text creates a world for audiences to enter through the

4. Roberts, *Nahum, Habakkuk, and Zephaniah*, 148.

performance, a world that includes actors, time, space, point of view, and standards of judgment. For this analysis, I will focus primarily on the actors.

Some performance critics call the people described and acting in a text "actors"; narrative critics would call them "characters."[5] In Habakkuk, we can discern three main actors in addition to the audience. *The first actor is the prophet, Habakkuk.* From our work behind the text, we know that a scribally trained prophet would be among a minority, an elite. He is not among the weak and dispossessed who struggle to eat and provide warmth and shelter when under crushing debt, some of whom are perhaps in the audience. He is well acquainted with wisdom teachings acquired in the process of education in the home, and he also seems acquainted with standard prophetic critiques against the wealthy and powerful.

Habakkuk changes as a character from chapter 1 to 2. He begins by questioning God and God's justice, even sarcastically. In chapter 2, however, he is prepared to wait confidently for God's answer. ". . . and let me keep watch to see what the Lord says to me, and what I will bring back concerning my rebuke" (2:1). He does not seem sarcastic anymore, but perseveres in his questioning, confident that God will explain.[6] Jeanette Mathews, following Terence Boyle, insightfully suggests that there is another way to perform this verse. "What I will bring back" could be performed as "What I will say back to God," implying Habakkuk will have another opportunity for questioning God.[7] His persistence before God pays off: he receives a vision that announces God's justice. As a result, he leads the audience in a psalm of praise. Finally, even as he reflects on the famine that often comes with invasion and vassalage, he announces his trust in God. In performance, the performer takes the place of the prophet through this movement

5. See discussion in Mathews, *Performing Habakkuk*, esp. 177–82.

6. "Indeed, perhaps we reveal the depth of our faith that God really does intend to keep his promises, when we come to him to ask him how long it will be before we see the fulfillment." Donald E. Gowan, *The Triumph of Faith in Habakkuk* (Atlanta: John Knox, 1976), 40.

7. Mathews, *Performing Habakkuk*, 119, esp. n. 1, which refers to Terence Boyle, *The Rhetoric of Taunt Language in Isaiah, Micah and Habakkuk* (PhD thesis, Dallas Theological Seminary, 2010), 178–90.

from sarcastic accusation to perseverant questioning to praise to trust in the midst of fear.

The second actor introduced is God, the addressee of Habakkuk's complaint, the giver of the vision, and recipient of the psalm. God speaks through the prophet, and so the performer must find ways to help the audience experience the difference between the prophet's voice and God's voice through the prophet. God speaks twice: first, in 1:5–6a and, second, in 2:2–12, 15–19. (I will argue below that God's speech ends at the announcement, "Behold, I am raising the Chaldeans!")

The third actor is the Babylonian king ("the Man" in my translation), who never speaks but who is described and addressed. As mentioned above, the prophet describes him in 1:6b–11 (third-person pronouns, "he," "his," "him"). In his rebuke of God, Habakkuk describes the Man as a fisherman who poaches God's fish, dragging them with net and fish-trap (1:15). He doesn't realize that it is the God of the universe who allows him to do this. Habakkuk mocks him as a fool who worships his net and fish-trap because they are profitable rather than recognizing the true source of his gain. But more than simple idolatry, Habakkuk describes the king as "slaying the nations without mercy" (1:17).

After discerning the actors, the next question is how they interact. Pronouns, especially "you," are central to this inquiry. God directly addresses the Man through the prophet in chapter 2.[8] God announces negative consequences ("woe!") for the Man using second-person pronouns ("you"). The address, "Will not your creditors suddenly arise / and will not the collectors for you wake?," could be a general indictment of wealthy who use loans to take property, but it becomes clearly applicable to the Man:

8. Following Mathews, *Performing Habakkuk.* This seems to make the most sense, although other readers take the "woes" to be examples of the taunts and riddles raised up by the people that the Man "gathers" and "collects." However, performing 2:2–19 as God's speech made more sense. First, understanding God as speaking the "woes" through the prophet is consistent with how Amos and other prophets use "woes." Second, if not God speaking, where does God's speech end? If it was the people and nations lifting up the "woes," it would make better sense to end God's speech earlier. However, "behold!" (*hinneh*) at the beginning of v. 4 sounds like a divine revelation and not simply the prophet's observation. Therefore, it makes the most performative sense to take the "he" of v. 6 to be the Lord ("he says," Heb *wĕyō'mar*).

> Because you plundered many nations,
> let the remaining peoples plunder you
> on account of human blood spilled and violence against the land,
> every village, and all who live in it. (2:8)

Habakkuk takes a general condemnation of the wealthy who build luxurious houses in "safe" places away from civil unrest that applied to the excesses of Judean leaders and turns it into an accusation of "counseling shame for your house," that is, bringing shame on the Babylonian house and the potential it had for glory. The house itself will accuse him, Habakkuk says:

> You counseled shame for your house
> to cut off many people. "Your soul is sinning,"
> a stone from a wall will cry out,
> and a rafter from the woodwork will answer it. (2:10–11)

Then, Habakkuk uses a general wisdom-inspired warning against getting neighbors drunk to shame them as a way to describe what the Babylonian king is doing with violence. A drunk spills wine on himself (imagine the picture), which is figuratively "the shameful shame on your glory" (1:16). Likewise, the Babylonian king has the violence of Lebanon on him like spilled wine. He has so devastated the land that beasts enter and terrify the people.

> For the violence of Lebanon covers you,
> and the devastation of beasts causes them to be terrified
> on account of human blood spilled and violence against the land,
> every village, and all who live in it. (2:17)

The audience also becomes a character in the performance. They are implicated in the lack of justice in the land. Habakkuk is talking about Judah when he first cries out to God about violence, sorrow, devastation, violence, strife, and contention (1:2–3). God's Instruction (Hebrew, *Torah*) is paralyzed and justice doesn't go forth, meaning that God's people, especially those responsible for administering justice, are "crooked." The audience must be sympathetic to this position, since Habakkuk does not directly accuse them. But it is likely that some in the audience might feel the sting of the accusation that "crooked justice goes forth," since Habakkuk has the social position of a scribal prophet with a network of runners who can communicate the vision.

The audience also may be implicated in the five "woes." I already noted that the topics of all five woes apply to the situation of the excesses of prosperity:

1. accumulating wealth by loans (2:6b–7)
2. building luxurious homes with wealth acquired through violence (2:9–11)
3. administrating cities and villages with violence and injustice (2:12)
4. encouraging drunkenness to shame a neighbor (2:15–16)
5. making idols and trusting them to teach (2:18–19)

Each of these could apply to powerful members of the audience. Three of them (1, 2, 4) include a second-person pronoun ("you") that seems to be address the Babylonian king. Are the other two implicitly addressing the king? In my performance, I try to create the sense that both the audience and the king are addressed by looking at the audience for the general "woes" and looking and then gesturing at the Man for second-person addresses ("you!").

The prophet directly addresses the audience three times. First, he interrupts the series of woes between the third and fourth with an interjection that sounds like he is marveling that God's justice still applies in an unjust world:

> Behold, is it not from the Lord of hosts
> that the earth will be filled
> with the knowledge of the glory of the Lord
> as the waters cover the sea! (2:13–14)

He refers to God in the third person and breaks the series of woes, perhaps suggesting that the audience respond with marvel as well.

The second time the prophet addresses the audience is to ask them permission to stand and wait for God's response to his rebuke. Three times the prophet says, "Let me":

> On my guard let me stand,
> and let me set myself on a siege mound,
> and let me keep watch to see what the Lord says to me. . . . (2:1)

The prophet is obviously speaking to the audience because he refers to God in the third person. By asking the audience permission to wait, the prophet yields power to the audience.

After singing the psalm with the audience, the prophet concludes with a final speech (3:16–19). He tells the audience that he is sick to his stomach and trembling after the vision, even after praising God as a victorious warrior in the psalm. Again, the prophet shows vulnerability to the audience, yielding power to them by showing his weakness. In doing so, he seems to join them in fear about the imminent invasion of the Babylonians and invites them to still praise and trust God.

Inquiry: World in Front of the Text

We can imagine that the first performances of the book of Habakkuk would be in a community setting, perhaps a village meeting place or even a courtyard of the temple. There are musicians standing by, having practiced and memorized the accompaniment for the psalm and the final instrumental piece. This first audience needs little description of the violence between Judeans and the excesses of the wealthy and powerful. A word or two triggers these memories easily. Likewise, fear of invasion by the Babylonians also comes easily and Habakkuk joins them in their vulnerability, drawing them into praise and trust in God in the midst of fear.

Audiences of later performances made different connections. For example, in the Jewish communities that used Greek translations (around 225 BCE), Habakkuk's view of the Babylonians seems to have been connected to Daniel. In Daniel 4, the Babylonian king Nebuchadnezzar is humbled and repents of his arrogance. This may explain why the Greek version of Hab 1:11 was performed:

> As then he will change his spirit,
> he shall pass through and make atonement
> [saying] his strength belongs to my God.[9]

Rather than continuing the violent and arrogant description of the Babylonians, the Greek version of Habakkuk reflects Daniel 4's experience that the arrogant king may change. The Hebrew version does not even consider this possibility, but is focused on expressing shock that God would add Babylonian violence on top of Judean violence.

In Qumran (around 50 CE), the *pesher* (or "interpretation") of Habakkuk is applied to a new situation. The "righteous person who is surrounded" is understood to be the leader called the "Teacher of Righteousness" at Qumran. Rather than the Babylonians, it is the Romans who have control of the land (called the *Kittim* in the Dead Sea Scrolls). Some aspects of the performance of Habakkuk at Qumran are radically different: the psalm of Habakkuk 3 is missing in the *pesher*. It was not a part of their commentary, but most scholars believe they knew of the psalm. What might this suggest about the way it was performed there?

Paul, the follower of Jesus (also around 50 CE), made Hab 2:4 central evidence in his letters to the Galatians (3:11) and Romans (1:17). In both these letters, he writes, "the one who is righteous shall live by faith," which matches neither the Hebrew nor the Greek versions of this passage. With this subtle shift, he creates ambiguity: Is it the righteous person's faith or God's faithfulness? As Mathews suggests, "through this ambiguity the quotation now serves the dual claims of Paul that the gospel reveals God's own righteousness and is salvation to everyone who believes."[10] For Paul's audience, the slight shift in performance yields new effects.

As the Masoretes transmitted the Hebrew text, they also performed it in ways consistent with their own theology. They may have been uncomfortable with Habakkuk's rhetorical statement in 1:12, "My God

9. Ibid., 189.
10. Ibid., 191.

of holiness, you never die!," both for its sarcasm and raising the possibility of the death of God. So, they performed it as "My God of holiness, we shall not die," even though this makes little sense in context.

It was perhaps natural that the psalm in Habakkuk 3 would be lifted out of context and performed without the rest. A ninth-century-CE epic poem called "the Old English *Exodus*" included the "Song of Habakkuk" as a canticle after Moses' song Exodus 15.[11] The similarities between the two songs make this natural connection, but in its new context Habakkuk's song no longer is a response of trust after a vision of future judgment.

I prepared Habakkuk to perform for the congregation in Arizona that I have served since 2009. It is located in an urban core, where many struggle with unemployment, underemployment, mental health, and addiction. Some in our community struggle with violence and tragedy and wonder where God is in the midst of forces that seem beyond their control. The week before I began performing the text, 130 people were killed in terrorist attacks in Paris. One member of the congregation texted me the day after, "I came upon Habakkuk. This book is new to me, short, so I read the whole thing. My mouth dropped as I read. It was what had happened in Paris yesterday." Comments after the four performances confirmed that others took the violence in Paris to be the situation for hearing the performance of Habakkuk.

Formatting for Performance

As described in chapter 2, I use a format for my translation that helps me to internalize the words, gestures, and desired effects. I put one main verb on each line, with indented lines underneath for dependent clauses. Using footnotes, I explain translation decisions. Verse numbers and further line markers are on the left. Gestures and performance effects are marked using Microsoft Word's "Track Changes" features to show bubbles on the right side of the page. I

11. Ibid., 192; see 192–96 for other ways that Habakkuk has been performed.

use a grey box around interruptions and digressions in the text. For example:

The LORD to the audience:
5 All of you, look at the nations and pay attention!
And be profoundly astounded!
For a work is being worked in your days
—you wouldn't believe it if it was retold!
6 For behold, I am raising to the Chaldeans!

The surprise: God is behind the rise of the Babylonian empire

The Prophet to the LORD:
That hurtful and hasty nation?
the Man who marches across expanses of the earth

Pointing to stage left to spatialize and personify Babylonian king

to take possession of dwelling places that
are not his own?
7 He is terrible and fearful,
From him, his justice and his dignity go forth.

Sarcastic emphasis on "his" to distinguish from God's justice, dignity.

8 And swifter than leopards are his horses
and keener than the wolves of the evening.
And they gallop, his gallopers and his gallopers!

Imagination: Internalizing Habakkuk

I began internalizing Habakkuk about two months before I planned to perform it. Every performance critic has their own techniques for internalization (see some examples in chapter 2). The first part is memorizing the words, although internalization is the goal, not simply memorization. I begin one line at a time, saying it out loud over and over again. When I can remember one line without looking at the paper, I add a second line. I continue this process until I have a block, for example, Habakkuk's first speech to God (1:1–4). Tom and Amelia Boomershine call this "chunking." By breaking up the text into manageable chunks it is easier to memorize. Each day, I try to recite what I have memorized up to that point, even if I am unable to add anything new that day.

The next step is imagining the scene. Even as I am memorizing, I am visualizing the space. How will I communicate that the prophet is talking to God? How will I help the audience "see" the Babylonian king? How will I emphasize the anger and sadness of the prophet? As I recite the words, I am trying out different intonations, gestures, and facial expressions.

Through this process, I am going back to edit the translation. As I internalize the text, it becomes clear to me that certain phrases aren't effective in communicating the desired effect (see more below on this). In retranslating, I go back to the Hebrew, to commentaries, and to other translations to think about different ways to create an effect for the audience. This movement from imagination back to inquiry is critical—the process of performance criticism is not linear.

Also during the process, I imagine specific people with whom I have had experience and can somewhat predict their responses. How will they respond to each line? As I practice, I imagine their facial expressions. Where will I lose them? Where do I need to be more emphatic?

Then, I go to the spaces in which I will perform, in this case, a small classroom, a chapel, and a sanctuary. How loud do I need to be to be heard in the back? What range of tones works for the space? Where will I look and gesture for the Babylonian king that does not make someone in the audience feel like they are accused? How will I express the waiting for God's response in 2:1? How will I express the difference between the prophet's speech to God and God's speech to the prophet? For example, I decided to look up and use a higher-pitched tone for the prophet's speech to God and then move to the left and use a deeper tone and looking down and to the right for God. The movement from right to left worked in the classroom and chapel, but in the sanctuary I was limited by altar furniture.

Internalization not only includes memorizing the texts but the embodiment of the text: emotion, facial expressions, movement, gestures, imagining the "actors," and anticipating responses of potential audience members. When the text is internalized, it is possible to hold the whole text and experience in mind. It is possible to imagine beginning at any point in the text and to hear connections between words and phrases in one part and how they connect to other parts.

Intervention: Performance Includes Introduction and Follow-up Interaction

Performance is transformative for the performer, the audience, and the relationship between performer, audience, and culture. Performance intervenes into the ways we conceive of our culture, power relations, and identity.

Before the performance event itself, intervention begins with the relationship between the performer, audience, and situation. Audiences yield certain authority to performers through their attention, position, relationship, and sometimes by paying admission. Likewise, congregations, in general, yield power to their leaders by gathering for Bible study, worship, and other events where the leader speaks and directs the interactions of the event. These events are, by nature, enculturating. For example, Bible study not only develops knowledge of the biblical material but also a way of interpreting that material, a way of relating to each other, and an understanding of who each person is individually and the identity of the group. Culture, power relations, and identity formation may be exposed by asking questions such as, Is disagreeing with the text an option? Is the leader's word the final word on subject? How much interaction do people have between themselves?

I performed Habakkuk in November 2015 for four audiences.[12] The first was a small Bible study that meets regularly on Thursday mornings. The second was in an informal worship service on a Saturday. The third and fourth were regular Sunday worship services.

The congregation I serve has experienced my previous performances and so many of them already have an idea of what I am doing. There are always new people, however, who think that when

12. Videos of three performances are available at https://vimeo.com/145597835; https://vimeo.com/147891938; and https://vimeo.com/148034001.

pastors stand up to speak they are going to speak as themselves. I make some preparatory remarks to help the audience understand I will be assuming a *persona*. As I discuss more below, I also include any remarks to help the audience more quickly comprehend the situation. For example, when I performed Habakkuk, I introduced the event by saying,

> I will be performing the book of the prophet Habakkuk, which is a small book in a collection of twelve prophetic writings at the end of what we call the Old Testament. Habakkuk was a prophet around 600 BCE during a time of prosperity in Judah, which was the southern kingdom of Israel with its capital in Jerusalem. In this time of prosperity, the rich were becoming richer—and sometimes by using violence and threats of violence against each other. In the meantime, a tribe called the Chaldeans were gaining power in what is now modern Iraq. These Chaldeans would become the leaders of the Babylonian Empire that destroyed Jerusalem and its temple about twenty years after gaining power. So, imagine with me the prophet Habakkuk talking to God.[13]

Such introductory remarks should be considered part of the performance, establishing expectations for the event and relationships between the four elements of *performer*, *text*, *audience*, and *situation*.

To measure the *effect* of the performance, I used a variety of methods to engage audiences. Such follow-up should also be considered part of the performance event, as the further interaction between performer and audience also *enculturates*, *interprets the experience*, and *shapes culture, identity, and relationships*.

In the small-group Bible study (about fifteen people), we were able to engage in an hour of discussion about the performance. I share some of the results of this conversation in the section below.

For larger groups, I asked the audience to write some responses to five questions and then to take a few minutes to discuss the experience with the person sitting next to them. The five questions, printed on a half-sheet handout, were:

13. Each time I performed, I introduced it differently, usually reacting to a perceived inadequacy in the way I introduced it the time before. Performances are cumulative for the performer and for the audience. Each new performance interacts with previous performances in the minds of both the performer and members of the audience.

1. In the very beginning, Habakkuk sees violence and injustice in his own land, his own people against each other. What is God's answer to this problem?
2. How does Habakkuk feel about God's answer?
3. What is God's answer to Habakkuk's rebuke?
4. What feelings did you experience listening to Habakkuk?
5. Any other comments you want to make?

The first three questions are designed both to check comprehension and help the audience process the performance. For most audience members this was the first time they had experienced the prophet Habakkuk in any medium. How much did they comprehend? For example, did they understand that God's solution to Judean violence and injustice was to send the Babylonians to invade? How much did the experience simply wash over them and leave only emotional residue behind?

The fourth question is meant to get at their emotional responses to Habakkuk. If my inquiry and imagination have been accurate, then a performance of Habakkuk should evoke responses to the prophet's anger and rebuke to God that is transformed to resignation and trust.

The fifth question allows for an open-ended response. This yields power to the audience to be affirming or critical, or to offer other kinds of feedback about the performance.

Intervention: How the Audience Was Changed

In general, the comprehension questions showed that about half the audiences comprehended the basic points that (1) Habakkuk was complaining about violence and injustice in Judah; (2) God's solution was to raise the Chaldeans to invade; (3) Habakkuk rebuked God for adding violence and injustice; and (4) God assured Habakkuk that true justice still existed and would triumph in the end. Despite not fully understanding the flow or content of the book, the majority of the audiences experienced the emotions of Habakkuk—the anger expressed to God for raising the Chaldeans followed by expressions of trust and hope even in a fearful time.

To the first question, "What is God's answer to this problem?," half of respondents (52 percent) answered, "I am raising the Chaldeans," "Big trouble is coming for the wicked," "The violent nation is coming," or similar responses. The other half took the question to refer to the whole book of Habakkuk, responding with phrases like "Believe in God," "Be patient, God has a plan," or "Keep the faith."

Question 2, "How does Habakkuk feel about God's answer?," was fishing for emotion words. Almost all (92 percent) responded with emotion words that fit the text and performance, including "anger," "frustration," "hurt," "let down," "disappointed," "sad," "scared," "confused."

The third question, "What is God's answer to Habakkuk's rebuke?," demonstrated the audiences' difficulty summarizing Habakkuk 2. Half (50 percent) answered something like, "Big trouble is coming for violent people." Another group of people (15 percent) focused on the issue of delay: the violence and injustice was only for a limited time before God's justice would be done. A third group focused on the final verses, that God would "help us to walk" (15 percent). Many left this question blank.

Question 4, "What feelings did you experience listening to Habakkuk?," evoked fewer emotion words. Some (28 percent) did use emotion words such as "confusion," "awe," "sadness," "pity," "distress," "helplessness." An equal number (28 percent) did not respond with emotion words, but connected Habakkuk to world events with phrases such as, "Seems like what the world is today." Violence in the Middle East was brought up in some of these responses, including, "This message hits home today with all that is going on in the Middle East" and "It sure sounds like the evil of all that the ISIL terrorists are doing now." Interestingly, no one connected the theme of internal violence in the United States (e.g., there had been over 350 mass-killing incidents in the U.S.A. in the past twelve months). Some (9 percent) were angry with Habakkuk for questioning God, one accusing

Habakkuk of thinking only of himself and another that the prophet was not letting God take care of the situation. Finally, a small group (6 percent) experienced a call to live by God's teaching or to be righteous.

The fifth question was open-ended, "Any other comments you want to make?" The majority of the responses (42 percent) affirmed the performance, for example, expressing amazement that I could memorize it. (This is a common response to other performances, one that suggests some people become distracted by the memorization itself rather than allowing themselves to be immersed in the experience.) Some (15 percent) made expressions of trust in God, such as "God's Word will prevail," "All will be taken care of in His time," or "God will still love us." Others (11 percent) expressed sympathy for Habakkuk, such as "Hard to watch evil develop" and "Where is God now as then as evil takes over." Some (8 percent) had trouble following who was speaking, writing things like "I wasn't sure when God was talking to Habakkuk or if it was Habakkuk talking to God." Others (8 percent) expressed confusion at the whole experience. Memorably, one wrote, "The airplane is circling," implying that it was all over her head.

Intervention: What I Learned by Performing Habakkuk

There are at least five ways I was changed in the process of *preparing*, *internalizing*, and *performing* Habakkuk.

1. *Translation for effect.* I prepared to perform Habakkuk for a specific group of people. As I prepared the translation I had the tension between the text and the audience and their situation in mind. As discussed in chapter 2, James Maxey has urged a *paradigm of hospitality* that values *carefulness*, *authenticity*, and *transparency*.[14]

Carefulness means that the translator handles the text with care as it is brought into a new situation. I take this "care" to mean a close investigation of Habakkuk that I described above: the world behind, within, and in front of the text that examines the effects the text

14. James Maxey, "Alternative Evaluative Concepts to the Trinity of Bible Translation," in *Translating Values*, ed. Piotr Blumczynski and John Gillespie (New York: Palgrave Macmillan, 2016), 57-80.

has had in various situations. From my careful reading of Habakkuk, I discerned Habakkuk's plea for God to respond to violence and injustice within Judah and his shock that God would choose the Babylonians as God's tool to correct the errant Judeans. God responds to Habakkuk's shock and outrage with a calm and confident assurance that God's justice would be done in the end. He encouraged the audience to live faithfully, even as they waited for invasion and famine. I was trying to evoke these effects in my modern audiences. Even if they may not fear imminent invasion or famine, they could identify with the outrage over violence in our country and world and questions about God's role in "justice coming forth."

Authenticity refers to the attention translators give to their relationship to the host community and to that community's language and preferred medium. The audiences I worked with are used to my performing texts, using gestures, movement, more emotive tone than other audiences may deem appropriate for the Bible. We have a preexisting relationship that provides a context for clearer communication than if I were performing for an audience with whom I had no relationship. Most people in the audience, while somewhat aware of biblical traditions, had never heard of Habakkuk. I had to be sure that the translation used words and phrases that created appropriate effects.

After performing Habakkuk for a small-group Bible study, we took time to discuss the translation. For example, the NRSV and many other translations translate the final verse (3:19) as "God, the Lord, is my strength / he makes my feet like the feet of a deer, / and makes me tread upon the heights." This translation fails to create the effects of fearful person navigating a dangerous situation while trusting God. The previous verses (3:16–17) make it clear the prophet is anticipating invasion and famine—these are the "heights." They are dangerous and fearful places. The word *deer* brings to mind for some in my audience the cartoon deer Bambi—cute and not the effect this verse in Habakkuk calls for. So, I translated it, "The Lord, my Lord, is my strength. / God places my feet like a mountain goat's / and on my high places makes it possible for me to walk." The use of "mountain goat" and "possible to walk" brought to the audience's mind the appropriate connotations of an animal navigating difficult and fearful terrain with confidence.

Another word that I discussed with the Bible study group was the word *woe*, which provides the structure and some of the emotional punch of chapter 2. After the first time I performed Habakkuk, I asked them what the word *woe* meant to them in the performance. One person said vaguely, "It's bad, whatever it is." Another thought "look out" was the sense of the word. I told them that the word is usually associated with funeral laments or to get attention, although it is used a bit differently here to suggest that God's judgment would come upon the five groups mentioned. I presented some options and asked what they thought communicated this idea:[15]

> "Who do you think you are . . . ?" (*The Message*)
> "You are doomed!" (Good News)
> "What sorrow awaits. . . ." (The New Living Translation)
> "Big trouble is coming for. . . ." (Walter Brueggemann)
> "God's judgment is coming for. . . ."

They liked "You are doomed!" for its dramatic quality. But when I performed it that way, I felt too much like a street preacher. It was difficult to create the effect of a general condemnation of these practices, which would apply to people inside the community, as well as the specific accusation made against the Babylonian king. As a result, in my final performances, I used "big trouble" because it allowed the audience to fill in for themselves what that big trouble might look like as well as perhaps hear that the warning against unrestrained greed applies to their own behavior. As discussed above, the majority of audiences did not hear that Habakkuk may be critiquing insider's greed or violence, but applied the warnings to outsiders, and especially violence in the Middle East.

The last value of a paradigm of hospitality is *transparency*. Transparency preserves the otherness of the Bible and the otherness of

15. See Gowan, *Triumph of Faith*, 52–55, for a discussion of how to translate "Woe!" After excellent analysis, he chooses "Oh!," which seems a bit weak to me.

the host community. To create a transparent translation is to maintain an effect of strangeness. The biblical traditions can't be domesticated or made to affirm an audience entirely for who they are. It is always "other."

When translating Habakkuk, the strangeness is easily apparent to the audiences for whom I perform. The name "Habakkuk" signals strangeness in a U.S. context; his identification as a prophet further puts the text outside the realm of experience. I debated about translating "Babylonians" instead of the word "Chaldeans" in 1:6a, but decided that either way I would need to say something about Habakkuk's situation in an introduction. So, I preserved "Chaldeans" as a further signal of the text's otherness.

The otherness of the audience is another facet of transparency. By addressing the otherness of the text, we also help the audience to define themselves as distinct from the text. In preparatory remarks and in concluding discussion, it becomes more clear that the audience needs to distinguish between their situation and the situation of the text, to empathize with some aspects and to be free to distance themselves from other aspects. I mentioned above my desire to create the effect of hearing the "woes" as a word of warning for the audience's behavior, not only that of others. What I found in conversation after the performances, however, was that the audience almost uniformly took the woes (or "big troubles") to refer to someone else other than themselves. As much as I hoped to create the effect of condemnation of violence by Americans on Americans, many thought of the threat of ISIS and terrorism. The audience is other, no matter what effects I as a performer try to emphasize from Habakkuk!

We translate for *carefulness*, *authenticity*, and *transparency*, but the particular effects of performance are in the experience of the performer and audience.

2. A second insight I had by performing Habakkuk was that Habakkuk interrupts God's initial speech, right after God reveals, "Behold! I am raising up the Chaldeans" (1:6a). I found that verses 6b–11, which describe the Babylonian king, express the prophet's surprise and

horror that God would choose this man—the Man—to be an instrument of "justice."

In order to explain this insight, it will be helpful for the reader to see the way the text is usually divided.[16] Most readers have taken verses 5–11 as God's speech to the audience. Here are verses 5–7:

5a All of you, look at the nations and pay attention!

5b And be profoundly astounded!

5c For a work is being worked in your days

5d —you wouldn't believe it if it was retold!

6a For behold, I am raising the Chaldeans,

6b that hurtful and hasty nation,

6c the Man who marches across expanses of the earth

6d to take possession of dwelling places that are not his own.

7a He is terrible and fearful;

7b from him, his justice and his dignity go forth.

God's speech is usually taken to continue until ". . . for he gives credit to their god for his strength" (1:11). Whoever is speaking, it is clear that the Babylonian king is being described negatively in verses 6b–11.

The problem is that God's introduction is positive. God calls the audience and the nations to attention. God invites them to be astounded, which sounds like they will be impressed with the solution. God announces that this is a "work being worked in your days," as if it is a satisfactory response to Habakkuk's complaint. God sounds like a carnival barker ready to unveil the great attraction. And then: it is the Chaldeans! After building up the audience's expectation of a positive solution to injustice in Judah, I had trouble announcing that the Chaldeans as "hurtful and hasty" (1:6b). I tried to perform 1:6b–11 in two ways.

The first way was to perform as if God was speaking verses 6b–11.

16. Most scholars take recourse to source criticism to explain the strangeness of 1:6b–11. Gowan writes, "We admit that vss. 5-11 are no satisfactory answer to the complaint in vv. 2-4" (ibid., 36). See also Roberts, *Nahum, Habakkuk, and Zephaniah*, 94.

This is the typical way to read this passage. God is speaking descriptively of the Babylonian king in verses 6b–11, perhaps with regret. In this performance, God knows that the king is "terrible and fearful." God regrets the necessity of such a problematic instrument to bring justice to Judah. It is as if to say, "Yes, that hurtful and hasty nation—isn't that a surprise? But yes, he's the one." This solution emphasizes 1:6b–11 as an explanation of why they "wouldn't believe it if it was retold" (1:5). Every time I tried this way, it seemed incongruous. First, that God would suggest this is a solution to injustice in Judah and, second, that "from [the Babylonian king], his justice and his dignity go forth" (7b). This was Habakkuk's language for describing the Judean situation in 1:4, twice saying justice does not go forth. After this setup, saying that the Babylonian king's "justice goes forth" sounds sarcastic by any speaker, which makes it more consistent with Habakkuk's tone then God's. Furthermore, a sarcastic and regretful tone does not match the tone of God's second speech in chapter 2, in which God's justice is revealed as still operative.

The second way was to perform this section as if Habakkuk was speaking verses 6b–11. In this case, the prophet interrupts God, reacting in shock. Instead of a statement, I made 1:6b into a rhetorical question the prophet speaks in shock to God's revelation that God has raised up the Chaldeans: "That hurtful and hasty nation? The Man who marches across expanses of the earth to take possession of dwelling places that are not his own?" If the prophet is the speaker, it makes better sense of the description that God's tool is "terrible and fearful" and he sarcastically says, "[the king's] justice and dignity go forth," rather than the justice from God's Instruction that the prophet desires (1:4).

Performing the text helped to clarify who was speaking and how the two parts fit together. God's announcement, "I am raising the Chaldeans!" (1:6a), is the jaw-dropper that triggers the prophet's unflattering description of the king of Babylon in 1:6b–11. After the negative description, Hab 1:12–17 is then a natural progression: the prophet's explicit rebuke of God for choosing this "terrible and fearful" instrument. Therefore, the text coheres better if it is read as:

The Lord to the audience:

5a All of you, look at the nations and pay attention!

5b And be profoundly astounded!

5c For a work is being worked in your days

5d —you wouldn't believe it if it was retold!

6a For behold, I am raising the Chaldeans!

The Prophet to the Lord:

6b That hurtful and hasty nation?

6c The Man who marches across expanses of the earth

6d to take possession of dwelling places that are not his own?

7a He is terrible and fearful!

7b From him, his justice and his dignity go forth!

3. I learned that the prophet asks permission from the audience to wait for God's answer. Performing Hab 2:1 led to a fascinating insight: it created sympathy between the performer and audience and suspense as they together wait for God's answer.

> On my guard, let me stand,
> and let me set myself on a siege mound,
> and let me keep watch to see what the Lord says to me,
> and what I will bring back concerning my rebuke.

Since he refers to keeping watch for what the Lord says, Habakkuk seems clearly to be speaking to the audience. Why would he ask for them to "let him" do this? As I performed this passage, I found myself asking audiences to let me wait for God's response and people nodded their heads as if to say, "Yes, we want you to wait for a response. We will be patient as you wait." What was the alternative? Would the audience be angry at questioning God's justice? As described above, some audience members were angry at Habakkuk. In this case, asking permission acknowledged their feelings. Others sympathized with the prophet's desire to wait—wondering if God would answer.

This last understanding is what became clear to me in performance: the audience identified with the prophet's questions to God and also wanted answers—and wondered if God *would* answer. In several of the performances, I turned my back to the audience and assumed a prayer posture and allowed a minute or two to pass. I was aware of my own desire to get on with the performance, perhaps replicating the impatience of waiting for a response.

I tried to express a bit of surprise by translating 2:2 as "And the Lord *did* answer me and said. . . ." God used a chastising tone after Job rebuked God (e.g., Job 38:2, "Who is this that darkens counsel by words without knowledge?"). With Habakkuk, God sounds compassionate and reassuring: "The vision is still for the appointed time, . . ." More waiting will be necessary for the vision to be fulfilled, but perhaps it will be easier knowing that God heard and responded to the rebuke.

4. Fourth, I learned multiple performances are necessary for an audience. The first time a person hears the performance of a text, it washes over them. They experience the emotions, but are often unable to articulate much about the experience. For example, I learned that the audience did not experience the psalm as a response of confidence in God's justice, as I had intended. The placement of the psalm in Hab 3:2–15 suggests that it is a response to the announcement of the five woes and the announcement that God is in "his temple of holiness" (2:20). As I asked the question, "Why do you think we sang the psalm?," most people responded by saying things like, "Because you told us to." Some of the people, however, who had heard me perform it more than once answered, "to respond to God" or "to worship God." This suggests that multiple experiences are necessary to begin to engage more deeply with the effects of a text.

How do people *know* something? These reflections on multiple performances further emphasize that people know principally through emotions, then imagination, and finally intellectually. The first time people heard Habakkuk, they could articulate emotional responses but not basic comprehension of his message. For those who experienced more than one performance, they could increasingly imagine the scene and express what happened.

5. I learned that Habakkuk creates a real and, I suggest, helpful tension between confidence and fear, praise and resignation. In Hab 3:16–19, the prophet shows he is not satisfied with the song of praise. This encourages the audience to feel some ambiguity about the effects of singing the psalm. When I asked people how the prophet felt after singing the psalm, many said, "He didn't sound happy." This is not a surprising effect, but it is notable how the audience experienced the fear and resignation of the prophet to the coming invasion and famine. The song of praise didn't take away these emotions or the threat that motivated them, but perhaps was an example of "exulting in the Lord" and "rejoicing in the God of my salvation" in the midst of fear. The psalm does not eliminate fear or create a false sense of "everything will be OK." The performance maintained the tension between confidence and fear.

4

Performing Revelation

The book of Revelation has long captivated the imagination with vivid images, colors, sounds, and drama.[1] It has moved artists to create paintings, music, and sculpture. People have used it to speculate on the timing of cosmic events and to identify enemies of God. For better and, sometimes, for worse, the book of Revelation has been performed for many audiences and has influenced *culture, power relationships*, and *identity* since its first performances in first-century Asia Minor, what we now call western Turkey.

Inquiry: The World Behind the Text

The book of Revelation identifies itself as at least three things: a *letter* written by a Christian prophet to seven congregations, a *prophecy* (that is, a message from God), and an *apocalypse* (an unveiling of some mystery).

1. For further exploration of how Revelation has influenced art, music, and culture around the world, see Arthur W. Wainwright, *Mysterious Apocalypse: Interpreting the Book of Revelation* (Nashville: Abingdon, 1993); Gerald L. Stevens, *Revelation: The Past and Future of John's Apocalypse* (Eugene, OR: Pickwick, 2014); and Judith L. Kovacs and Christopher Rowland, with Rebekah Callow, *Revelation: the Apocalypse of Jesus Christ* (Oxford: Blackwell, 2004).

It is a *letter* that has many standard features of an ancient letter, including a "to . . . from" formula and a greeting, "Grace to you and peace . . ." (1:4; compare how Paul begins his letters, e.g., 1 Cor 1:1–3). Although many later performances have taken this letter to apply to a universal and timeless audience, Revelation does not address itself to all people in every time, but presents itself as a letter from a specific person (John) to specific groups (seven congregations) in time (the end of the first century CE) and space (the Roman province of Asia). We will inquire into their situation below.

Revelation also is a work of *prophecy*, a message from God. Some readers take the word *prophecy* to mean predictions of what will happen in the future. This is how some audiences throughout history have taken the book of Revelation. Prophecy, however, is better understood as a message from God that may involve the future but is relevant to the present. A prophet is the person chosen to deliver that message. John clearly believes that the message from God is relevant to audiences of his time. He begins by announcing that his audience will be blessed by hearing it and keeping it: "Blessed is the one who reads aloud the words of the prophecy, and blessed are those who hear and who keep what is written in it; for the time is near" (1:3). John sounds like a prophet. He uses words and phrases that evoke memories of other biblical prophets, such as Daniel and Zechariah. For example, after the letter opening, he interrupts the flow with an exclamation:

> Look! He is coming with the clouds;
> every eye will see him,
> even those who pierced him;
> and on his account all the tribes of the earth will wail. (1:7)

Which reminds some audiences of phrases from one of Daniel's visions combined with one of Zechariah's prophecies:

> As I watched in the night visions,
> I saw one like a human being
> *coming with the clouds* of heaven.
> And he came to the Ancient One
> and was presented before him. (Dan 7:13; emphasis mine)

> And I will pour out a spirit of compassion and supplication on the house of David and the inhabitants of Jerusalem, so that, when *they look on the one whom they have pierced, they shall mourn* for him, as one mourns for an only child, and weep bitterly over him, as one weeps over a firstborn. (Zech 12:10; emphasis mine)

Even if an audience can't recall Daniel or Zechariah, John sounds like a prophet. Even if they recognize that he is using them in a different way than Daniel or Zechariah intended, John captures the expected sound and experience of prophecy. He builds up his authority as a messenger of God. Milman Parry showed how oral tradition reuses prior performances in formulas and set pieces (see chapter 1). John uses prophetic language as building blocks for a new performance.

Finally, Revelation is presented as an *apocalypse* (1:1), that is, an "unveiling" or "revelation." It is the first document we have that is labeled that way (although there are passages in Daniel and Jewish literature outside the Bible that sound similar). Revelation unveils the cosmic drama that lies hidden behind the mundane social drama of its time. From appearances, it looks like the Roman Empire is bringing peace and trade throughout the Empire. John sees the hidden reality. His visions unveil that the Empire is really like a Beast (with a capital "B") serving Satan and making war on God's people. The great city of Rome is revealed to be a jeweled prostitute who drinks the blood of the saints. The "apocalypse" pulls back the curtain to show that the peace and prosperity is a sham, and a temporary one at that.

The location of the audience is made clear by identifying them as "the seven churches that are in Asia" (1:4). By referring to them as "in Asia," John brings to his audience's mind that Asia is the name of their Roman province. It recalls the power relations of the Empire that carved up geography into political regions to be managed by imperial governors under the emperor himself. Local civic leaders in these cities were often eager to show their loyalty to the emperor with temples, statues, sacrifices, festivals, and parades.[2] John's revelation unveils these as idolatry, which wouldn't be a surprise to people who knew

2. Steven J. Friesen, *Imperial Cults and the Apocalypse of John* (New York: Oxford University Press, 2001).

Judaism or the Hebrew Bible. God's people can't worship a statue of the emperor (13:14)! It is a false prophet that promotes such worship, even if they bring fire down from heaven (13:13) and make it seem like the statue can speak (13:15).

The situation is more complex than worship of the emperor. The seven "letters" of the glorified Jesus to the congregations (chapters 1–3) highlight the real problems that are *inside* Christian congregations in Asia. Some Christians are compromising with the idolatry of the Empire. Five out of seven congregations have faced or will deal with false teachers, that is, false from John's point of view. These so-called false prophets would probably have identified themselves as faithful Christians, but in the performance of Revelation their identity is transformed. Those who would teach Christians to eat meat sacrificed to idols are called false prophets. Those who teach that the Empire is peaceful and can be traded with are false prophets. These last two points are worth further elaboration.[3]

3. Steven J. Friesen, "Satan's Throne, Imperial Cults and the Social Setting of Revelation," *Journal for the Study of the New Testament* 27, no. 3 (2005): 351–73. See also Craig R. Koester, *Revelation: A New Translation with Introduction and Commentary*, The Anchor Yale Bible Commentaries (New Haven: Yale University Press, 2014), 85–103.

We know from other writings (Acts, 1 Corinthians, and Romans) that eating food sacrificed to idols was a controversial issue for early Christianity. Some Christians argued, "All other gods were false gods, and so what difference does it make if we eat meat that was sacrificed to Zeus? We know there is only one true God" (see, for example, 1 Cor 10:19). They may have remembered Jesus saying, "All foods are clean" (Mark 7:19; see Acts 10:15). Other Christians argued that to eat meat sacrificed to idols was to participate in idolatry (1 Cor 10:20). The basic social meaning of sacrifice is to have a meeting with a god; to eat meat sacrificed to Zeus is to socially acknowledge and meet Zeus. When Christians met in Jerusalem in about 50 CE to discuss how to include Gentiles in the primarily Jewish Christian movement, they decided to require them to give up eating food sacrificed to idols (Acts 15:20). Paul, however, counseled Christians in Corinth to eat the meat at an unbeliever's house as long as it didn't scandalize other people's faith (1 Cor 10:27–28). Even with the decree from the Jerusalem council, Christians were not of one mind on the subject of eating idol food.

John enters this controversy by labeling proponents of idol food "false prophets" and "false apostles." In his visions, they are connected to Balaam, a prophet who led Israelites astray, and Jezebel, Ahab's pagan queen who killed Israel's prophets. From John's point of view, there can be no compromise with those who teach that eating idol food is acceptable. They are comparable with the "Beast of the Land" who encourages worship of the Beast (the Roman Empire) and even Satan (13:11).

But the condemnation of emperor worship and eating food sacrificed to idols are not sufficient to explain the long and complex structure of the book of Revelation. These issues are introduced in the first three chapters and Jesus' condemnation could have been enough. What is it that is revealed in twenty-two chapters of Revelation? What is hidden at the beginning of the book that is unveiled by the end?

The real revelation happens at the end of chapter 17. The surprise: the great city (Rome) is the Great Prostitute described on the back of the Beast. (I will refer to her as "the Woman," with a capital W, just as in the last chapter I used "the Man" for the Babylonian king.) Unique to chapter 17, John explains the symbols, while most in Revelation go unexplained. The seven heads are unveiled to be seven hills on which the prostitute sits. They are also seven kings, one has fallen and will return. The ten horns are ten kings who will serve the Beast for a little while. The punchline comes at the end: "The Woman you saw is the great city that rules over the kings of the earth" (17:18). In the first century, there was only one "great city" in audience's memory: Rome. Why would this be a surprise to John's first audiences?

Rome seemed decked with wealth and prosperity—and thus the blessing of God in the view of some Christians.[4] John represents this position when he is amazed by the Woman clothed in purple and scarlet clothes, gold, jewels, and pearls: "When I saw her, I was greatly amazed" (17:6). His guiding angel condemns an attitude of amazement towards her prosperity: "Why are you so amazed? I will tell you . . ." (17:7). The fall of Babylon (Rome) described in chapter 18 also focuses on people who profited from Rome's luxury, including merchants, shipmasters, and seafarers. Some of these may have been involved in the seven congregations: "Alas, alas, the great city! All who had ships at sea grew rich by her wealth!" (18:19; see 18:11–19). The theme of Christians who are profiting from trade with Rome is highlighted in Jesus' letter to Laodicea, the last city to be described (3:14–22). There, Christians are encouraged to trade with Jesus for clothes, wealth, and medicine rather than other unnamed trading partners (3:18). It is not revealed until chapters 17 and 18 that Rome is the trading partner to be rejected in favor of Christ.

Some Christians also seem to believe that the Roman Empire is benign toward Christians. Up to the time of John's visions, they seem to be right. John is only able to point to one Christian who has been killed, whom he lifts up by name: "Antipas my witness, my faithful one, who

4. For more on the theme of God's wealth to overshadow Rome's wealth, see Robert M. Royalty, *The Streets of Heaven: The Ideology of Wealth in the Apocalypse of John* (Macon, GA: Mercer University Press, 1998). On how John compares Rome to the New Jerusalem, see Barbara R. Rossing, *The Choice Between Two Cities: Whore, Bride, and Empire in the Apocalypse* (Harrisburg, PA: Trinity Press International, 1999).

was killed among you" (2:13). If many Christians were dying in Asia Minor, John would have said so. But only one has died and John raises Antipas's name as if on a protestor's sign to warn that many more are to come. The problem, therefore, is that most Christians don't think Rome will be violent. For this reason, John emphasizes the violence of the Beast and Woman toward the saints: "[The Beast] was allowed to make war on the saints and to conquer them" (13:7); "I saw that the woman was drunk with the blood of the saints and the blood of the witnesses to Jesus" (17:6). But this violence is anticipated and not yet real.

John slowly reveals that Rome is the idolatrous, violent Woman because many Christians believe that the Empire is not violent toward Christians and so they can safely and lucratively trade with her. This helps to explain the structure and content of the book. First, he presents images of outlandish wealth in God's throne room and fear of God's judgment. The strategy is to overwhelm Christians' love of Roman wealth and to create fear of an unidentified power that will kill Christians (chapters 1–11). Then, he reveals the enemies of God one at time: first Satan, then the Beastly Empire, then the prophetic supporter of the Beast (chapters 12–13). He announces judgment on their idolatry (chapters 14–16). None of this is a revelation: the audience would not be surprised by Satan and his forces killing believers and promoting emperor worship. The new character and the real revelation is in chapter 17: the Woman who sits on the Beast is the one "drunk on the blood of the saints." She represents Rome, the Great City, who seemed so beautiful and benign. The difficult command in chapter 18 is the call for believers to "come out of her" (18:4). The painful unveiling is the response to Rome's destruction by those who trade with her. Less of a surprise is the heavenly hallelujahs over Rome's destruction. Long-awaited justice follows: the grisly devastation of the Beast's forces, then the false prophet, the Beast, and the Dragon, Satan, and finally God's judgment of all people (chapters 19–20). Last, Christians are given a vision of the true wealthy city, the New Jerusalem, with whom they should desire trade and through whom healthy power relationships will heal the world (chapters 21–22). In the end, Revelation offers confidence in God's healing and restoring power over fear of imperial power and even of God's judgment.

Performing Revelation should reflect the pacing and focus of this structure. In the first eleven chapters, a performance slowly reveals the hidden, glorious throne room of God as well as fear of God's judgment. It quickens with the threat of God's enemies and announcement of their imminent destruction. It slows with surprise and sudden dawning as the Woman and her true identity are exposed—and some in the audience begin to realize their complicity in her idolatrous pleasures. Grief at her destruction and fear of being destroyed with her motivates the audience to change their behavior and loyalties. Finally, and with lingering hope, the New Jerusalem is described and the audience is drawn in to become those who worship before the throne of God and the Lamb. In this way, the primary effect of the performance is to release the audience from their loyalties and pleasures in the Empire in order to witness publicly to what God is doing.

Media plays an important role in Revelation. Although we usually think of it as a "book," this English word in the twenty-first century conjures pages sewn together, glued to a spine, and bound with covers. This picture is closer to what would be called a "codex" in the first century.[5] But Revelation is more appropriately understood to be a "scroll" made most likely of parchment, the stretched, scraped, and dried skins of sheep or goats. The author of Revelation, who calls himself John, is very conscious of the medium.

John expresses two concerns about how the scroll will be handled. On one hand, he is concerned that it will be sealed up, never to be widely read. The angel who guided his revelation commands at the end of the visions, "Do not seal up the words of the prophecy of this scroll, for the time is near" (22:10). He perhaps fears it will be lost with all the other esoteric prophecies that seem to emerge in every age. Wide circulation fits the purpose that he presents in the very first

5. Colin H. Roberts and T. C. Skeat, *The Birth of the Codex* (New York: Oxford University Press, 1987).

verses. By writing his visions and asking them to be read aloud (i.e., performed), he makes it possible for everyone to experience what he has experienced and to be moved by the performance to "keep what is written in it" (1:3). If the book is sealed only for a group of insiders, it will fail in its purpose, which is to transform people's lives. In other words, Revelation is for everyone, not just for the elite few.[6] *This is an intervention into culture, power relations, and identity.*

John has a second concern about the medium of scrolls. If it is going to be widely read and disseminated, it will likely be copied, re-performed many times, and changes in performance written into new copies. As we discussed in chapter 2, it was common for scribes to expand or contract the performance of a text based on the needs of the audience and the situation. John explicitly warns against it, as if a command from Jesus himself:

> I warn everyone who hears the words of the prophecy of this scroll: if anyone adds to them, God will add to that person the plagues described in this scroll; if anyone takes away from the words of the scroll of this prophecy, God will take away that person's share in the tree of life and in the holy city, which are described in this scroll. (22:18–19)

In this way, Revelation co-opts the audience to be the guarantors of later copies of the scroll. In other words, he is saying, "You who hear this: if you hear a different version than what you heard today, that person is going to have the kind of divine and cosmic trouble described here!" By reinforcing God's power over the text, the text itself reinforces the audience's power over the performer and its performance. The audience yields power to the performer, and they can withhold that power by disapproval of the performance. The audience checks the performer using their memory of prior performances. The text uses Jesus' name to command the consistency of the performance, even when different performers, audiences, and situations may call for additions and expansions. The performer, then,

6. Bruce W. Longenecker calls this the "democratization of prophecy," which is a bit of an anachronism but makes the point strikingly. Longenecker, *Rhetoric at the Boundaries: The Art and Theology of the New Testament Chain-Link Transition* (Waco, TX: Baylor University Press, 2005), 119.

has to negotiate between these forces: conserving the tradition to avoid the audience's disapproval and the threat of divine wrath while innovating where needed and possible to reach the desired effects.

John's visions refer directly to four other media and their cultures: *songs, administrative lists, monumental inscriptions*, and *slave markings. Songs*, specifically hymns and chants, are a critical part of Revelation. When the four living creatures began to sing, "Holy, holy, holy, the Lord God the Almighty . . ." (4:8), many audiences will bring to mind a familiar song based on Isaiah 6:3, "Holy, holy, holy is the Lord of hosts; the whole earth is full of his glory." Would the performer shift from speaking to singing these lines? Perhaps the performer used a tune familiar to the audience. (This is the way I perform it.) Even if not, many audiences would have the music beginning like a soundtrack in their minds. As memories of music surface, memories of prior performances rise with them. Perhaps most importantly, the medium of music brings emotion with the dynamics of the notes and sound. It is a grand feeling evoked with singing "Holy, holy, holy," being swept up with the prophet into the majesty of the throne room of God, singing with all the angels and the heavenly host. Early Jewish and Christian music also unified communities, creating a sense of common identity. Finally, singing in these communities evoked a sense of worship of God. Singing was one of the primary ways to express proper devotion and relationship with God. Within this media culture, the songs in Revelation would have greater emotional impact if sung. For example, "You are worthy, our Lord and God . . ." (4:11); "You are worthy to take the scroll . . ." (5:9–10); "Worthy is the Lamb that was slaughtered . . ." (5:11); and "To the One-Sitting-on-the-Throne and to the Lamb . . ." (5:13), each heighten emotion, create identity in community, and express devotion to God.[7]

A second kind of medium important to Revelation is *administrative lists*. Leaders of cities and governors of regions kept lists of people for administrative purposes and list of people's activities.[8] The first kind of

7. For more on the impact of hymns in Revelation, see K.-P. Jörns, *Das hymnische Evangelium. Untersuchungen zu Aufbau, Funktion und Herkunft der hymnischen Stücke in der Johannesoffenbarung* (Gütersloh: Mohn, 1971) and Koester, *Revelation*, 126–30.

list is a *citizenship list.* For example, a list of citizens would be used to plan and collect taxes, to provide a list of eligible voters in democratic Greek cities, and to select potential members of councils or to pay for special projects. These citizenship lists showed who belonged and had rights and responsibilities to the community. These lists could be read aloud to call attendance at a meeting or in a court.

A citizenship list is a way a group yields power. They put power into the hands of those who control the list and it shapes the identity of those on the list. It includes some and excludes others. It gives rights to some and denies rights to others. The list shapes identity; for example, you are a free citizen, in part, because your name is on the list.

When John sees visions of the "Lamb's scroll of life," his audience would likely imagine it as similar to this kind of list. In John's vision, the Lamb controls the list, which includes people from every tribe, language, nation, and people (5:9). People's names are included or erased in the scroll of life (3:5). Like citizenship, there are certain expectations of behavior if your name is on the list. Someone with their name in this scroll will not worship the Beast, who opposes God and God's people (13:8; 17:8). Having your name in the scroll of life means you won't be thrown into the lake of fire (20:15) but will be included in God's City, the New Jerusalem (21:27). Power, in this way, is truly given to the Lamb, and the identity of those on the list is shaped.

The other kind of list is a *list of deeds,* a history of a kingdom organized by events and people associated with them. This is perhaps the kind of list that Esther's audiences thought of when they heard that the Persian king read when he had insomnia:[9]

> The king could not sleep, and he gave orders to bring the book of records, the annals, and they were read to the king. It was found written how Mordecai had told about Bigthana and Teresh, two of the king's eunuchs, who guarded the threshold, and who had conspired to assassinate King Ahasuerus. (Esth 6:1–2)

8. For detailed discussion about citizenship lists, lists of deeds, and other kinds of heavenly books, see Leslie Baynes, *The Heavenly Book Motif in Judeo-Christian Apocalypses 200 B.C.E.–200 C.E.* (Leiden: Brill, 2011).
9. Ibid., 59.

Closer to Revelation's time, Livy (d. 17 CE) was commissioned by Emperor Augustus to write the history of the Romans, with lists of names and deeds that could be celebrated or vilified when the history was performed. Similar to these annals and histories, John's vision of judgment refers to a "scrolls of deeds": "And I saw the dead, great and small, standing before the throne, and books were opened . . . And the dead were judged according to their works, as recorded in the books" (20:12). As with the annals and histories that would be performed to celebrate people and deeds, vilify enemies, and cure insomnia, Revelation's scrolls of deeds provide the basis for judgment.

Revelation also refers to *monumental inscriptions*, a third medium important to understanding the media culture behind the text. Inscriptions on massive stones were the billboards of the ancient world, perhaps not always read by the masses but always understood. When supporters of Emperor Augustus engraved large stones throughout the Empire (especially in Asia Minor where John sent his visions), word of mouth spread the stories of the emperor's deeds. One person who reads it tells twenty others, for example, how the inscription announced that the emperor brought peace to the Empire. Another kind of public inscription is relevant. In several cities throughout Asia Minor, archeologists have found inscriptions in Jewish synagogues with names of contributors engraved on the walls.[10] Those who could read would be asked, "Whose name is that?," and the name—and their deed—would be performed for a new audience.

John's audiences would likely remember the engraving of names on monuments and civic buildings when Jesus announces that he will make the faithful in Philadelphia into "pillars of the temple of our God" (3:12). Just as faithful patrons had their names engraved on the walls of synagogues to show how they helped build and maintain it, those from Philadelphia who hold fast under pressure will have their names engraved as "pillars" of God's temple. To be a pillar meant having their

10. Paul R. Trebilco, *Jewish Communities in Asia Minor* (New York: Cambridge University Press, 1991). See also Friesen, *Imperial Cults*, 30–31.

reputation raised in the community every time it is performed for new members of the community.

Finally, Revelation refers to the practice of *branding* or *tattooing slaves*. This medium also has a performative element. To see a slave's tattoo is to know that person's identity: they are owned. It is performed when someone sees it and says, "A slave of the emperor!" or "A slave of Cicero!" Identity is shaped by the slave's master; the power of the slave is the power that their master yields. Some slaves could wield considerable power. Consider Tiro, the slave of the Roman politician and philosopher Cicero. Cicero had yielded significant power to Tiro to run his estates and properties, and to direct both freedmen and slaves. Tiro could write and read fluently. He likely was not branded or tattooed. On the other end of the spectrum, slaves working in the mines would work with no protection from cave-ins, oxygen deprivation, or other risks but might be tattooed in order to prevent them from running away.

Within this social situation, John sees writing on the forehead of both Christians and others. Jesus announces to believers in Philadelphia: "I will write on you the name of my God, and the name of the city of my God, the new Jerusalem that comes down from my God out of heaven, and my own new name" (3:12). In a later vision, the mark on the believer's forehead is called "a seal" that shows they are included among the people of God (7:5–8; 14:1) and protected from the ravages of the plague of locusts loosed by the fifth trumpet angel (9:4). The seal on believer's foreheads is contrasted with the mark of the Beast that is placed on people's forehead or right hands and is necessary in order to conduct trade (13:16). This is a part of the subtle unveiling that one of the central issues is Christian complicity in Roman trade. Like a slave brand or tattoo, all people will receive a mark of ownership. The question posed by this medium to the audience is: Whose slave will you be? God's or the Beast's? By trading with Rome, are you allowing yourself to be marked by the Beast? As a mark on the forehead, the slave mark is a public announcement, a performance when read. Symbolically, the seal or mark represents how a person demonstrates their loyalty through their actions. In this way, John asks through a performance of Revelation, "What is on your forehead for others to see?" or "How do your actions demonstrate who your master is?"

Inquiry: The World of the Text

A performance of Revelation creates a world for audiences to enter, following John through a series of visions. In this world, John is one actor among other actor, including the One-Sitting-on-the-Throne, Jesus, interpreting elders and angels, the Dragon, the Beast, the False Prophet, the Woman "Babylon," and many others. There are fantastic settings in heaven and earth. John's use of time is worth comment, as well as the standards of judgment established as the story unfolds.

Revelation has too many characters to describe in detail. I will name a few and refer the reader to James Resseguie's *The Revelation of John: A Narrative Commentary* for more detailed inquiry.[11]

John is the first actor we meet, and the one that provides the point of view for telling the story. He is a prophet (22:9), but distances himself from the smaller group of apostles (21:14; see 18:20). He goes to great lengths to align himself *with* the audience and not *over* the audience. He is a "brother who shares with you in Jesus, the persecution, the kingdom, and the patient endurance" (1:9). He admits ignorance (7:14). He is amazed by the Woman's wealth (17:6). In these ways, he restructures power relationships to position himself with the audience in yielding power to God and the Lamb in the performance.

The One-Sitting-on-the-Throne, or *God*, is the primary character in Revelation. God is referred to so many times by the phrase "the one sitting on the throne" that I treat it as a proper name. From that throne come lightning and thunder (4:5) and the river of the water of life that waters the tree of life that will heal the nations (22:1–2). The title "One-Sitting-on-the-Throne" contrasts with all others that would claim to sit

11. James L. Resseguie, *The Revelation of John: A Narrative Commentary* (Grand Rapids: Baker, 2009), 103–59. See also David L. Barr, *Tales of the End: A Narrative Commentary on the Book of Revelation* (Santa Rosa, CA: Polebridge, 1998).

on the throne, that is, to be the center of power relationships. Some have made Satan a throne in Pergamum (3:13). Satan, the Dragon, gives his throne to the Beast (13:2). The Woman sits on the Beast like it is a throne (17:3) and claims she sits as a queen (18:7). But these are nothing compared to the throne in heaven. The One-Sitting-on-the-Throne is the one who truly rules. He speaks only twice as bookends to the performance, which gives gravity to his voice (1:8; 21:5). It is helpful to imagine the throne room to one side of the performance area; I will discuss this below.

Jesus, likewise, is referenced by other names and descriptions that produce a kaleidoscope of characterization. The revelation is from Jesus; the title of the book is "The Revelation of Jesus Christ," and so he is the source of its message. He is described in the letter opening as "the faithful witness, the firstborn from the dead, and the ruler of the kings of the earth" (1:5). John sees him as "one like the Son of Man," clothed in robe, golden sash, and in many other ways evoking images from Daniel's visions (1:13–20). Gestures help draw out the vivid imagery of Jesus. For example, I move my hand along a line out of my mouth to the audience when he is described with "a sharp, two-edged sword proceeding from his mouth" to demonstrate that it is the sword of his words, rather than a typical sword that is drawn from a scabbard. The performer, who assumes the persona of John in performance, must choose whether to fall down or gesture toward the ground or simply modulate the voice to help communicate the awe of this initial vision (1:17). Much more could be said about the characterization of Jesus: as Lamb, as overlapping in many ways with God, and so on. Richard Bauckham and James Resseguie have insightful observations for readers who wish to pursue this topic.[12]

The *interpreting elder* and *angel* are characters worth describing here because John interacts with them. Therefore, the performer must interact in some way with these characters. These interactions draw the audience's attention toward significant moments when John and

12. Richard Bauckham, *Theology of the Book of Revelation* (Cambridge: Cambridge University Press, 1993).

(by extension) the audience become more active participants in the experience. No longer is John merely watching passively. First, he weeps when no one is found to open the scroll (5:4). One of the twenty-four elders diverts him from weeping to seeing the Lion who is a Lamb (5:5). John acts obediently: he looks and sees the Lamb take the scroll, the event that triggers cascading praise throughout the cosmos (5:6–14). Next, when John sees a great multitude in white robes praising God, an elder quizzes him, "Who are these?" John is forced to admit he is ignorant and the elder is the one who knows (7:13–14). John shows humility and a desire to learn. The voice that called John to the heavenly throne room later commands him to take the little scroll from the hand of the mighty angel and eat it (10:8–9). John obeys and suffers a stomachache even as he prepares to prophesy again (10:11). In the final scenes, he is corrected several times by the interpreting angel. He is amazed by the wealth of the Woman and told not to be (17:6–7). He twice bows down to the interpreting angel and twice told not to do that (19:10; 22:8–9). By helping the audience visualize these characters, the performer brings to life the elders and angels who guide John and, by extension, the audience. John humbly admits his ignorance and mistakes to the audience, and in this way invites the audience to admit their ignorance and mistakes. By example, John leads the audience to grow in understanding and to change their behavior.

The characters that oppose God and God's people include the *Dragon* (Satan), the *Beast from the Sea* (or simply "the Beast"), the *Beast from the Land* (later revealed to be the "False Prophet"), the *Woman Called "Babylon,"* and *kings* that support the Beast and the Woman. The Dragon and the Beast are described in great detail. It is helpful to make a careful mental picture, terrible in imagination, so that the performer is able to by facial expressions and intonation express fear and awe.

The *setting* alternates between heaven and earth. John begins on earth, on the island called Patmos. In prayer ("in the Spirit"), he sees Jesus as "the One Like a Son of Man" who dictates the seven letters to the congregations. Quickly afterwards, John is swept up to the heavenly throne room where he observes the events following the opening of the seals and the blowing of the trumpets. He looks down on heavenly actions affecting earth, for example, the four horsemen being sent to earth after the opening of the first four seals. Although John's vantage point is heaven, much of what he sees happens on earth; for example, after the fifth and sixth trumpets in chapter 9, the action is only on earth (the shaft of the bottomless pit opens after the fifth trumpet and angels are released from the Euphrates after the sixth). John moves to earth beginning in chapter 10, as he sees "another mighty angel coming *down from heaven*" (10:1) and putting one foot on the sea and another on the earth. He walks over to take the scroll from this angel, implying he is also on earth. In chapter 12, he seems to be looking up in the heavens to see the Woman Clothed by the Sun (12:1). This earthly vantage point seems to continue through the end of the book, when he sees the New Jerusalem coming down from heaven (21:2). But the location is ambiguous: he also hears the One seated on the throne; one of the seven angels with the bowls comes over to him. Is he on earth seeing the New Jerusalem coming down? Or is he in the heavenly throne room looking down as it descends? In performance, it is almost automatic to gesture "coming down" with the hands in a way that implies that the heavenly court is up and the earth is down, as if performer and audience are midway between heaven and earth.

I have found it helpful to visualize the throne room on one side of the performance space and the Dragon and the opponents of God on the other side of the room. This allows me to gesture and look at one space or another and help audience track the many characters and events in the book. I picture the heavenly throne room to the audience's right (my left), with the four living creatures, twenty-four elders, angels, and later events associated with the throne room (e.g., the Great Multitude described in 7:9–17). To the audience's left (my right), I visualize the Dragon, the Beast, the False Prophet (a.k.a. the Beast from the Land), and the Woman. When I mention one of these characters, I look and gesture to that side of the room.

John's use of *time* is sometimes difficult to track. Did he experience all these visions on a Sunday morning or are these visions spread out over many years and then compiled and arranged in Revelation? To take chapter 7 as one example, John writes, "After this I saw," to introduce a vision of 144,000 (7:1) and then introduces a second vision of a great multitude (7:9) with a similar phrase. How long "after" in John's experience did these visions come? This is examining time from John's perspective.

From the perspective of the events described by the visions, how are they related? Is the vision of the 144,000 in chapter 7 describing past, present, or future? The location of this vision is ambiguous. On the other hand, the vision of the great multitude (7:9–17) is in the location of the throne room and seems to describe a distant future after believers have come out of a great tribulation. Later in Revelation, similar themes are connected with the New Jerusalem coming down out of heaven (21:3–4). Is the vision of the great multitude a vision into that future? Does the vision of 144,000 then refer to the same time?

Other visions seem to describe events that his audience could identify as their present time; for example, the rider on a white horse with a bow could be easily identified with images of Parthian archers that threatened the eastern edge of the Roman Empire (6:1–2). Others are so strange as to be imagined as symbols of the future; for example, demonic locust horses who sting people but don't kill them (9:1–11). Locust swarms, they could imagine. Humans on horses, they could imagine, perhaps as Parthians again. But to combine them as demonic locust horses, this is a fearful mixture that hasn't happened. Similarly, John and his audience are only aware of one Christian who has died: Antipas. But John anticipates many to be killed because of their testimony to Jesus (20:4). Past, present, and future seem sometimes blurred together in horrific imagination.

The blurry and confusing handling of time is not unraveled in performance. When referring to events that seem to be related to the coming of the New Jerusalem and the healing of the nations (22:2), I turn and gesture toward the throne room, that is, the audience's right, to draw attention to the work of God, or up toward heaven and the New Jerusalem. When describing the horrific events that seem to be past, present, or near future, I gesture to the Dragon to draw attention to the consequences of following the enemies of God.

By this up/down and right/left division of spatializing the book, I try to make it easier to experience the standards of judgment created by the story. As I noted earlier, the story is trying to draw the audience out of loyalties to the lifestyle created by imperial trade and meals where idol food is eaten. The audience is caught in the middle. By drawing increasingly clear dividing lines, the performance invites the audience to choose who they will fear, worship, and serve, with whom they will trade, and to which prophetic voices they will listen.

Inquiry: World in Front of the Text

There's far too much in front of the book of Revelation, especially in Western culture, to describe here. For those who want to investigate further, Arthur Wainwright's *Mysterious Apocalypse* is a good introduction. Gerald L. Stevens's 2014 book, *Revelation: The Past and Future of John's Apocalypse*, is the most current and comprehensive study. Christopher Rowland and Judith Kovacs's commentary places emphasis on the history of interpretation (especially artwork) as it explores the text in detail.

For our purposes in the twenty-first-century English-speaking world, a particular performance of the book of Revelation has been popularized. "Dispensationalism" is a label given to one way the book has been read to predict the future.[13] Beginning with John Nelson Darby in the nineteenth century, Revelation was read to divide history into seven "dispensations" that end with the rapture of believers from earth to heaven, seven years of bloody tribulation for those "left behind" as an antichrist rises, concluding with the return of Christ and the bloody end of all those who refuse to follow him. This way of

13. Popularized most recently by the "Left Behind" series of novels and related products. For introduction to dispensationalism and a critique, see Barbara R. Rossing, *The Rapture Exposed: The Message of Hope in the Book of Revelation* (New York: Basic, 2005). For the way this reading of Revelation has influenced the power relations of Israelis and Palestinians in the twentieth century, see Timothy P. Weber, *On the Road to Armageddon: How Evangelicals Became Israel's Best Friend* (Grand Rapids: Baker, 2005).

"performing" Revelation has been popularized to the point that many audiences are aware of it without knowing where it comes from.

Performers also should be aware of the ways the book of Revelation imitates the gender violence of its time.[14] On coins and inscriptions, the Roman Empire routinely pictured conquered cities and peoples as naked women. One striking image shows a conquering Nero, depicted as an armored male, dragging a naked Armenia by her hair. John shows the ten kings committing similar violence against the Woman in Rev 17:16–17. John implies this is God's purpose: "And the ten horns that you saw, they and the beast will hate the Prostitute; they will make her desolate and naked; they will devour her flesh and burn her with fire. For God has put it into their hearts to carry out his purpose by agreeing to give their kingdom to the beast, until the words of God will be fulfilled." After I performed Revelation for an audience in 2014, one member of the audience said she almost threw up when she heard these verses. We took time to discuss her and other audience member's reactions to the gender violence in Revelation and how to work to end violence against women in our time.

As a result, almost every performance of Revelation needs to be prefaced with a description of first-century historical realities that will help a modern audience. First, a modern audience should understand that the book made sense to its original audiences and didn't need to wait two thousand years for people to connect images and symbols to their "real" references. By describing the first-century situation—for example, in the way I described it above in the "Inquiry: World Behind the Text" section—audiences will better understand the message for that time and draw more appropriate conclusions for our time. Second, performers may have to address the gender violence, perhaps in introduction, post-performance discussion, or even modifying the performance to diminish these effects. In "Intervention" below, I will

14. This does not mean that all audiences hear gender violence in Revelation. Compare Tina Pippin's exposé of Revelation and Vitor Westhelle's describing Brazilian women who found it liberating. Tina Pippin, "The Heroine and the Whore," and Vitor Westhelle, "Between the Colonial and the Postcolonial: A Reading from Brazil," both in *From Every People and Nation: The Book of Revelation in Intercultural Perspective*, ed. David Rhoads (Minneapolis: Fortress Press, 2005), 127–45 and 183–99, respectively.

discuss further the performer's responsibility to guide audiences toward healthy responses.

Inquiry: The Contemporary Audience

The "World in Front of the Text" also includes the intended audience for the performer. Who will experience the performance of Revelation? What effects are desired for this audience?

Over the last ten years, I have performed Revelation in part or in whole over a dozen times for different audiences. For the purposes of discussion here, I will compare two different audiences that experienced my performances of Revelation. The first was a group of students and faculty at a seminary in November 2006. The second audience was members of a Christian congregation in January 2014. Comparing these two performances reveals the different dynamics of performance with different audiences and situations.

The first performance was for about twenty students and faculty at a seminary in Illinois in November 2006. Most were familiar with the book of Revelation. A few had taken a course on Revelation; others had studied the Roman Empire in other courses. They had studied the Bible academically and approached it analytically. In general, as I prepared to perform, I believed I could assume they would understand common biblical symbols, such as the color white being a symbol of purity, and that they would easily imagine Revelation was speaking to another time and place. I thought they would need less introduction for these reasons. I also believed this audience would receive the performance less emotionally and more analytically. (I was wrong about many of these assumptions, as I'll explain in the "Intervention" section below.)

The second performance for reflection here, in contrast, was to about 125 members of a Christian congregation in Arizona in January 2014. Many of them told me they tried to avoid the book of Revelation based on what they heard. They had heard about the scary imagery and predictions of future disasters. In pre-performance surveys, they expressed fear of God's judgment and of the performance itself. Some of the audience were familiar with dispensationalism and other "futurist" interpretations that look for contemporary fulfillment of the visions. I thought I would need an introduction of the situation for Christians in the eastern Roman Empire to help connect symbols with that time and place. I could not assume that the audience would understand the symbols used; I had to decide whether to introduce explanations in the introduction or the performance. In the end, I decided to elaborate on some of the symbols in the introduction. For example, "seven" is commonly understood to represent the number of completion; horns a symbol of power; so, seven horns represent complete power.

Translation for Performance

I used a similar translation for performance for both performances (see a sample of Revelation 17–19 in appendix B). In this translation, I try to emphasize the sound of words that create effects, for example, "practicing promiscuity" for translations of the Greek roots of *porneu-*, which is the basis for the words translated in the NRSV as "sexual immorality" and "prostitute." This *p*-alliteration creates memorable sounds in English that help audiences connect the teachings of the Nicolaitans, "Balaam," and "Jezebel" to the Woman. To make the connection with the situation of the Roman Empire more clear, and the contrast between God's rule and Roman rule, I translated *basileia* as "empire" rather than the more conventional "kingdom." Roots of *thlipsis* are usually translated "ordeal" or "tribulation," both nebulous words for many modern audiences. I instead translated them as "pressure" or "public pressure" to connect with the introduction's description of public pressure for Christians to participate in social meals where idol meat was offered and in the prosperity of trade with the Empire. By translating words in a way that create "sound threads," I tried to connect images in visions to make the situation for the audience more clear.

I also added explanations when it seemed that John was providing extra assistance for his audience. When John translates a Hebrew word into Greek to help his Greek-speaking audience, such as the name of the angel of the bottomless pit, I included an English translation: "They have as king over them the angel of the bottomless pit; his name in Hebrew is Abaddon, and in Greek he is called Apollyon, *and in English, Destroyer*" (9:11).

John's Greek is unique. Sometimes his grammar sounds like that of a child or non-native speaker. In English, if we heard someone say, "John gave *she* the coat," we would correct the speaker to say, "You mean, 'John gave *her* the coat.'" Most translations smooth over his awkward use of cases, for example, translating Rev 8:9 as "a third of living creatures in the sea died" (NRSV). But the grammatical case of the word translated as "living" doesn't match "creatures." It stands out in Greek like the word *she* in "John gave she the coat." How can we create the effect of awkwardness in English and what might it mean?[15]

Following the work of G. K. Beale and Allan Callahan, I suggest that John sometimes uses awkward grammar to draw attention to allusions in the Hebrew Bible and to motivate the audience to change.[16] Revelation 8:9 is better represented in English as "a third of creatures in the sea—things having lives—they died!" or even more clearly as "a third of creatures in the sea—things with lives created by God—they died!" to express the allusion to the creation of sea creatures in Gen 1:20–21. John shows his shock at so many of God's creatures dying, and by the awkward grammar invites his audience to identify with them. Both sea creatures and humans have lives (Greek: *psychai*). Both praise God. In the book of Revelation, both are dying as a consequence of human sin. Grief over God's creation is one reason for John's audience to change, and a reason to bring out the effects of his unique grammar when we can identify its potential effect.

15. For more on this subject, specifically dealing with Rev 8:9, see Peter S. Perry, "'Things Having Lives': Ecology, Allusion, and Performance in Revelation 8:9," *Currents in Theology and Mission* 37, no. 2 (April 2010): 105–13.

16. G. K. Beale, *The Book of Revelation*, The New International Greek Testament Commentary (Grand Rapids: Eerdmans, 1999), 101. Allan D. Callahan, "The Language of the Apocalypse," *Harvard Theological Review* 88 (1995): 453–70.

Volume

One issue to consider in preparing a text for performance is volume. What indications are given in the text? Revelation gives many cues about the intended volume of direct speech. I have divided the volume into five levels:

1. A normal conversational voice indicated by forms of "say" and similar words (e.g., 1:8). Speech between individual characters would be lower than between an individual and a group (e.g., 7:13–17 is conversational compared to 1:8 as proclamation).
2. The larger sound of a group indicated by plurals, such as "they said" (5:14; 6:16; 10:11; 19:3; 22:17) and perhaps a bit louder when a group "cried out" (18:18, 19; cf. 12:2).[17]
3. "A loud voice" is used twenty-three times in nineteen verses (1:10; 5:2, 12; 6:10; 7:2, 10; 8:13; 10:3; 11:12, 15; 12:10; 14:7, 9, 15, 18; 16:17; 19:1, 17; 21:3). "A strong voice" is used once in 18:2. I also have assigned to this level the voices of the four living creatures during the opening of the seals, based upon the combination of the verb "say" with the comparison "like a voice of thunder" (6:1; cf. 10:3).
4. This "loud voice" is amplified another level by the size of the character (5:2), comparisons to trumpets (1:10; cf. 4:1) or lions (10:3); by the verb "cry out, shout" (7:2, 10; 14:15; 18:2; 19:17).
5. Multiple loud voices amplify the volume to the loudest (6:10 with "cry out"; 11:15; 19:1).

The performance space and audience will suggest different ways to express the changes in volume. For example, when giving the impression of a group crying out, the performer may choose to use gestures to communicate the increase in volume rather than simply raising her or his voice. A smaller space will allow less modulation of volume, while a larger space may be more appropriate for louder voice. The performer wants to be sure that even at the softest volume, people throughout the room can hear.

17. The Greek *krazō* emphasizes the loud volume in every aspect of this word.

Gestures

The book of Revelation offers many opportunities to consider gestures that *decrease the audience's effort and increase desired effects.* Some gestures may include: lifting the right hand when the right hand is mentioned (e.g., 1:16), cupping the ear when John hears (e.g., hearing the songs of the four living creatures, 4:8), or putting a hand over one's eyes when John sees (e.g., "After this, I looked . . ." 4:1). When characters ascend or descend, when doors are opened or closed, foreheads marked or sealed, these are opportunities for gestures depending on the performer, audience, and situation. Gestures may assist the audience to experience the effects of the performance more vividly.

Pronouns are especially important to comprehension. When the audience is addressed as "you" it holds their attention; a gesture of a finger or open hand may increase this effect. Demonstrative pronouns such as "this" and "that" may be more easily understood with pointing at the object (even if imaginary) or movement of the hand. For example, Jesus says to the congregation in Thyatira, "to the rest of you in Thyatira, who do not hold this teaching . . . ," has the effect of separating some hearers from those who follow the teachings of the prophetess he calls "Jezebel" (2:24). By gesturing "this" away from the group, it visually separates the current audience from that position. (I gesture toward the place I later will imagine the Dragon, Beast, and false prophet as a visual connection.)

Gestures can also help the audience experience the shape of the visions. For example, when John shares his vision of the glorified Jesus in chapter 1, he sees head and hair, eyes, feet, and a sharp, two-edged sword. Gesturing toward an imaginary head and feet of Jesus helps the audience see it themselves. A gesture of the hand from the lips toward the audience while saying, "and proceeding from his mouth was a sharp, two-edged sword," assists the audience in understanding it is not a literal sword but his words that cut.

Humor

While many may think that the book of Revelation is grimly serious, there are many humorous moments, mostly due to John's willingness to expose his weakness. The audience naturally will think of John as a prophet, as a leader, and as other than themselves. If the performer plays these passages for humor, the performance mirrors the text's attempt to help the audience feel empathy and identification with John—and better to accept the message of changing lifestyle and loyalties. Here are five examples of humor in Revelation.

First, when John sees the glorified Christ, he comments, "When I saw him, I fell at his feet as though dead." Jesus, however, humorously points out that he knows what it is to be dead. "But he put his hand on me, saying, '. . . *I* was dead, and see, I am alive forever and ever . . .'" (1:17–18). The twofold point seems to be that John really doesn't know what it is like to die and, even more, if Jesus has been raised from the dead, why should John fear even death?

Next, one of the elders asks John a question, "Who are these clothed in white, and where have they come from?" (7:13). John acts like a schoolboy caught in a pop quiz: "Lord, you know!" (7:14), implying "I don't!" In other visionary tales (e.g., Dan 7:16–20), the prophet asks the questions. Here, John confesses his ignorance to both the elder and, through the performance, to the audience.

Once again, John shows his ignorant eagerness when he hears seven thunders. "I was about to write, but I heard a voice. . . ." But a voice from heaven stops him, "Seal up what the seven thunders have said, and do not write it down" (10:4). This simultaneously portrays John both as overeager and also obedient and open to correction—just as his audience should be.

Another opportunity for the audience to laugh at John and see him corrected is when he tries to worship the interpreting angel. After being told to write the vision of the fall of Babylon, he falls down at the angel's feet. The angel immediately stops him: "Don't do that!" (19:10). John doesn't learn easily, it seems, because he does it a second time

(22:9). Like his response to the elder, this presents the Seer as a bit clueless—which gives the opportunity for humor, but also to witness his humility and willingness to be corrected.

Although not directed at John, I have found it amusing that 1,260 days and forty-two months are mentioned separately though they are actually equivalent. For example, the nations are allowed to trample on the holy city for forty-two months; but the two witnesses have authority to prophesy for 1,260 days—the same amount of time (42 x 30 = 1260; see Rev 11:2–3; 12:6). Commentators don't pick this up, but it's a funny inside joke.[18] These numbers reflect an apocalyptic time period, 1,260 days from Dan 11:3; 12:6. By converting days into months, the Seer, however, sets up a comparison of the numbers forty-two and 1,260 that makes the witnesses testimony more impressive, even if one knows they are the same time period. When performing, 1,260 sounds so big compared to forty-two, but the insider knows they are exactly the same!

Sarcasm

Some of Revelation's characters sometimes sound sarcastic, that is, mocking characters who are not changing their lives according to the standards of judgment.

- To Sardis: "You have a name for being alive, . . . but you are dead!" (3:1).
- To Laodicea: ". . . You say 'I am rich. I have prospered. I have no need.' But you do not know that you are wretched, pitiful, destitute, blind and naked." (3:13; see the similar language by the Woman Babylon in 18:7.)
- "But don't harm the wine or olive oil" (6:6) sounds sarcastic when contrasted with staples such as wheat and barley that hungry people would want to protect.

18. For example, Brian K. Blount, *Revelation: A Commentary*, New Testament Library (Louisville: Westminster John Knox, 2009), 205.

- "The demons and idols . . . which cannot see or hear or walk" (9:20). Of course, statues can't hear or walk; even pagans acknowledged that. This is typical prophetic sarcasm about foreign idols (e.g., Isa 42:17–18; 44:9–20).
- "Who is like the beast? Who can fight against him?" Through the first twelve chapters, John has already established the silliness of this question. It is a part of the "clueless dwellers of earth" theme, characters who ask silly questions that are obvious to the audience (e.g., 9:20, as mentioned above). I perform it in a sarcastic falsetto like the people of Laodicea claiming they are rich (3:17) and Babylon who says she rules like a queen (18:7).

Sarcasm has the effect of separating those who are in the know from those who are clueless, those who are being mocked from those who are being honored. In this way, John encourages his audience to choose to change and be among those who are knowledgeable and honored.

Sadness

In order for his audience to give up their pleasurable lifestyle of social meals and trade with the Empire, he has to help them grieve their loss. As we discussed earlier, John shows characters being sad about losing their wealth and trade with Babylon (18:9–19).

John is also sad about no one being found worthy to open the scroll (5:4) and about the slaughter of people and creatures (for example, see the above discussion of sea creatures). "Slaughter" is a significant and emotional term used to describe the Lamb (5:6, 9, 12; parodied by the Beast in 13:3, 8), and later to witnesses to Jesus (6:9) and all slaughtered by Babylon (18:24). John suggests that the slaughter of Jesus and his witnesses can be seen in the same vein as those slaughtered by Babylon after the red rider is released (6:4). I perform the announcement that the red rider causes "people to slaughter one another" with a sense of sadness and regret that God has allowed this rider to continue to perpetrate violence similar to what Jesus and the witnesses suffered.

By comparing these experiences of sadness, the audience is allowed to grieve their change in lifestyle while assuming the greater grief over the potential loss of life (human and nonhuman) if people don't change their ways.[19]

Formatting for Performance

As with Habakkuk, I use a format for my translation that helps to internalize the words, gestures, and desired effects. I put one main verb on each line, with indented lines underneath for dependent clauses. Using footnotes, I explain translation decisions. Verse numbers and further line markers are on the left. Gestures and performance effects are marked using Microsoft Word's "Track Changes" features to show bubbles on the right side of the page. I use a grey box around interruptions and digressions in the text. For example:

19. For other examples of sadness, consider: ". . . many people died from the waters because they were made bitter" (8:11). John does not describe these as "those dwelling on the earth" but simply "people"—a category in which a believing audience would see themselves. Also, after the two witnesses are killed, "those dwelling on the earth" celebrate: ". . . even sending gifts to one another" (11:10). John uses an emphatic "even" to express sadness and disbelief that those dwelling on the earth would celebrate the death of God's witnesses.

c) Interruption: An oracle

7a Behold — *Different voice: an oracle in real time.*
b He is coming with the clouds,
c and every eye will see him,
d even those who pierced him;
e and for him all the tribes of the earth will beat (their chests). — *Gesture: beat chest as 18:9*
f Yes. Amen.
8a "I am the Alpha and the Omega," — *God's voice—only here and 21:5-8. Whisper*
b says the Lord God,
c who is
d and who was
e and who is coming, the almighty.

d) Audition: Setting and commission

9a I, John, your brother and partner (with you) — *Negative*
in public pressure and empire and
endurance in Jesus, — *Positive—say last and with adversative sense (but)*
b was on the island called Patmos
c because of the Word of God, (which is) the testimony of Jesus. — *Tie to name of white rider*
10a I was in (the) spirit on the Lord's day,
b and I heard behind me a loud voice like a trumpet — *Gesture behind, hand to ear*
11a saying,
b "What you see, — *Loud voice (volume +1)*
c write on a scroll
d and send (it) to the seven congregations:
to Ephesus, — *For each city, gesture to pre-designated section of audience.*
and to Smyrna,
and to Pergammum,

Imagination: Internalizing Revelation

As discussed in chapters 2 and 3, *internalizing a text is more than memorizing the words but making the text and effects a part of the performer*, just as John eats the little scroll before going to speak before peoples, nations, languages, and kings (10:11). I internalized the book over about a six-month period. Almost five out of seven days each week, I spent about a half hour repeating chunks of text out loud while trying out different gestures and visualization of the text. After I could repeat the whole book over a week (it takes me about 100 minutes to perform the whole book), I would repeat chunks while I walked or drove. (It did earn me some strange looks!)

It was in the process of internalizing Revelation that I developed the idea of visualizing the heavenly throne room to my left (the audience's right) and the Dragon and his forces to my right (the audience's left.) I also began to act as if I was receiving some parts of the vision in the performance itself; it made sense as I suddenly said, "Look! He is coming with the clouds . . . ," to act as if I could see Christ coming in the clouds in that very moment and that I was inviting the audience to see with me. I thought this might create the added effect of feeling that Christ's coming was so imminent that we might experience it during the performance. (This effect was confirmed by discussion after several performances.)

I also found that internalization deepened my awareness of interruptions in the text. I had a hard time remembering them! For example, I found myself misplacing or forgetting the three woes proclaimed by the eagle: "Woe, woe, woe to the inhabitants of the earth, at the blasts of the other trumpets that the three angels are about to blow!" (8:13). John tries to make the eagle's cry easy by putting it as a transition after the shorter (and quicker) series of the first four trumpet plagues and before the longer (and slower) fifth and sixth trumpets. Even knowing that, it was easy to be in the flow of the trumpet blasts and blow right to the fifth trumpet. Several times in practice, I placed the second woe following 9:21 (the end of the sixth trumpet event) rather than 11:14 (after the two witnesses). The beatitude in 14:13 is another interruption I easily forgot. "Blessed are the dead who from now on die in the Lord" comes between the three angels in midheaven and the four figures who reap the harvest and vintage of the earth. These difficulties in memorization highlight for me that these elements are interruptions to the flow of the story. It also highlights the way these interruption become more prominent to both performer and audience by breaking the flow of the performance.

The longer elements that I call "digressions" (e.g., 7:1-17; 10:1—11:13), however, are not so difficult to remember because of their length and significance.[20] These visions digress from the expected series of seven seals and seven trumpets, between the sixth and seventh element. They focus on characters with whom the audience may identify. In this way, the digressions help the audience overcome the fear of God's judgment and persecution by Roman forces in order to confidently witness to God and the Lamb.

Intervention: Ethics and Introduction

When thinking through performance as intervention, two initial aspects are important to consider: *ethics* and *introduction*.

First, the *ethics* of performance. As discussed in chapter 2, any performance is an intervention into culture, power relations, and identity. The performer asks: What are my goals in this performance? What goals are healthy and appropriate for this audience? What goals may be an abuse of the power yielded by the audience to the performer? What in the current culture or power relations may produce unanticipated and undesirable effects?

Second, I learned that an *introduction* is necessary to minimize assumptions and reach desired goals. Looking back at the notes from my first performance in 2006 for a group of about twenty seminary students and faculty, I admit to being naïve about the effects of performance. I used a minimal introduction when I performed and

20. On the function of these digressions see Peter S. Perry, *The Rhetoric of Digressions: Ancient Communication and Rev. 7:1-17 and 10:1—11:13* (Tübingen: Mohr Siebeck, 2009).

gave little insight into how the performance should be conceived or the audience's role. I was known to the audience, as was the content of Revelation, so I assumed I did not need to introduce myself as a credible exegete or give an overview of the text. In my mind, I had divided the audience into seven groups, each correlated with one of the seven congregations. As I performed Jesus' "letter" to each, I looked at that group, shook my finger at them when Jesus commanded them to repent, and threatened consequences with my eyes, voice, and posture. As a result of this performance and not giving enough information, some found it to be very disturbing. I remember one person in "Thyatira" pushing back in the chair as they were accused. In discussion, several audience members wondered if I was trying to recreate a first-century experience of the text. Several commented about the violence they felt like they experienced, and lingered even though I intended the hope and confidence of Revelation 21–22 to have lasting impact. A few were able to articulate what they thought the performance might mean for today, but they also were the ones who had already studied Revelation. To put it mildly, this performance was a growing experience.

As an intervention into culture, what kind of culture does a performance of Revelation try to create today? For the performance in January 2014, I used a pre-performance survey as one way to get at that topic. The survey questions were:

1. Have you read through the book of Revelation before this class?
   Yes No
2. What are your feelings about the book of Revelation?
3. What do you think the purpose of the book of Revelation is?
4. What questions do you want to be sure are answered?

On one level, I was trying to get a clearer sense of the audience's prior experience and assumptions about the book of Revelation. I also was trying to begin the conversation about the purpose of the book of Revelation and the ways it uses emotional language and imagery to persuade the audience to change. Did they anticipate that the performance would affect them emotionally? Did they anticipate that the performance would change them?

From the returned surveys, I learned that 62 percent of the audience had read through the book of Revelation before. For the second question on their feelings, confusion was the dominant emotion (29 percent responding with answers such as "confused," "hard to understand," or "uncertain"), with a small number (6 percent) answering "fear" or "wonder." The majority gave no answer to this question (50 percent), which suggested to me that they were unable to identify any feeling toward the book.

Of those who answered the question about the purpose of the book, the majority thought the purpose was to inform people about what would happen at the end times (27 percent answered "predict future," "predict end times," "give God's plans," or "inform about second coming."). Small numbers thought the purpose was to compare to today's times (2 percent) or to scare us (2 percent). Some admitted they had no idea (10 percent) and the majority left the question blank (51 percent).

The final question was meant to evoke other issues that the book of Revelation may have raised. Of those who answered, a majority wondered how important the book of Revelation really was today (15 percent). Interestingly, the people who questioned its relevance left the purpose question blank, suggesting that they couldn't think of a purpose for the book in general or a reason to read it today. Some wanted to explore the symbolism of the book (4 percent). Others reinforced the need to understand its purpose (4 percent). Others asked questions that revealed a futurist or dispensationalist reading, asking questions like, "What will the sequence of the end times be?" (2 percent), "What will happen to us?" (2 percent), "Will the Jews be saved?" (2 percent). Others asked more general questions, such as "Was it inspired?" (2 percent) and "When was it written?" (2 percent). As with the other open-ended questions, many left the space blank (48 percent).

After the survey, I introduced the performance by inviting the audience to imagine themselves at a gathering of seven Christian congregations, each sitting with others from their city. I told them there was an active controversy among Christians about whether or not they should eat food that had been sacrificed to idols, and that not everyone in the room agreed on what to do. Some of them should imagine themselves as merchants and members of guilds who trade with the Roman Empire, while others struggle to have enough food to eat or clean water to drink. My intention was to set their minds to be sensitive to Revelation's persuasive strategy.

Intervention: How the Audience Was Changed

Following the performance, they audience completed another survey before our large group discussion. The questions of the post-performance survey deliberately mirrored the first survey to allow for comparison and discussion of the effect of the performance.

1. What were your feelings as you experienced the book of Revelation?
2. After the performance, what do you think the purpose of Revelation is?
3. What questions did the performance of Revelation raise for you?

Of course, I would like to report that everyone understood it perfectly and made all the connections described in my introduction. That didn't exactly happen. Of those who responded, the majority (21 percent) wrote that they felt "awe," "wonder," "moved," "repentant," or similar words. Some were still confused (8 percent) while some who thought they understood the book now felt confused (7 percent). Some were troubled or upset by the performance (4 percent). One person felt like it was a "fantasy movie," while another thought "the story seems like someone on drugs." Half (50 percent) did not respond to the question. After further conversation, I found that many were still processing the experience and weren't able to immediately articulate any response.

On the purpose of Revelation, the majority of people who answered said some form of "repent and believe" (19 percent). Some thought the purpose was to "scare a person to death" (6 percent). Others were looking for grace or forgiveness, and couldn't find it, writing questions such as "Where's grace?" (4 percent). A few still thought the purpose was to tell us what the second coming of Christ would be like (2 percent).

The performance raised many questions for the audience, mostly about specific symbols such as the thunder and lightning, slavery, the "new name," and blood (23 percent). Others asked about John's identity and the identity of the seven congregations (6 percent). Some still asked about the relevance of Revelation (8 percent). Others responded to the violence, asking something such as "Why all the blood (or death)?" (8 percent).

In summary, the performance itself did change the audience. Many were moved emotionally by the performance to use words like "awe" or "wonder," which would suggest they experienced it as if they were transported to the heavenly throne room. Almost all who thought the book was predicting future events, such as the coming of Christ, were persuaded by the performance that it was about something else, especially as a call for the audience to repent.

As I found in performing Habakkuk, the experience washes over many audience members with more emotional than intellectual effects. Many were unable to articulate thoughts immediately after the performance. People were better able to articulate how they *felt* than what they *thought*. This seems to confirm my suspicion that Revelation is making a largely emotional argument with its audiences, trying to move them away from fear of persecution to awe of God's judgment and confidence in God's saving power that will enable them to change their luxurious lifestyles and witness to God's work through the Lamb. This audience was able to articulate the fear and awe, but not the specific ideas or changes that Revelation urges.

Over the next three weeks, the group met three more times to discuss the book of Revelation. Through this time of closer study (less emotional, more intellectual), the audience was able to articulate some of these ideas, especially the importance of witnesses to God and the Lamb.

Intervention: What I Learned by Performing Revelation

There are at least ten ways I was changed in the process of preparing, internalizing, and performing Revelation.

1. I am more convinced that a longer and more detailed introduction to a performance of Revelation is necessary. Each time I have performed, I have given a slightly longer introduction, but have been hesitant to say too much. My preference has been to let the performance speak for itself. Since most audiences respond emotionally to the material, however, I think it would be useful to give an overview of the emotions they may feel and why John presented them this way. Some may argue that this biases the audience toward particular responses, which is true. People's responses to Revelation are so colored by their preconceptions of the book, however, that it is naïve to think that they aren't already biased. Rather, it seems wise to share my understanding of the book's purpose and argument more explicitly in order to help the audience process my performance with less effort. The next time I perform Revelation, I will use a detailed introduction similar to the section "The World Behind the Text" above. Not every biblical text will need a lengthy introduction, but I suggest that the length and detail of the introduction should be proportional to the existing conceptions and confusion in the audience.

2. Performing Revelation has confirmed the analysis that Revelation 17–19 is the unveiling that the audience didn't see coming. The time, pacing, and emotion underline this conclusion. It requires about a fifth of the total time to perform the description of Babylon and the responses of various groups to her destruction. The pacing slows down with the more detailed descriptions—for example, the list of cargo no longer traded with Babylon (18:12–13). Emotions are explicitly

expressed by human characters, crying out, weeping, mourning, and throwing dust on their heads (e.g., 18:17–18).

This section of Revelation also has some of the most violent and misogynistic images, which evoke revulsion in me as the performer as well as in the audience. It is difficult to perform "the ten horns and the beast that you saw, these will hate the whore and will lay her waste and naked, and will consume her flesh and burn her with fire" (17:16). I have learned that discussing the violence, especially against women (even if symbolic), is important to an ethical performance of Revelation. Many audiences need opportunity to express their emotional responses and condemn violence against women in the first century as well as the twenty-first century.

3. I now read many of the "Behold!" (Greek, *idou*) statements in the text as a vision *given in performance.* For example, the striking interruption of Rev 1:7–8 ("Behold! He is coming in the clouds . . .") makes the most sense if the performer presents it as if they are receiving the vision in that moment. The performer becomes a conduit and embodiment of the visions, so that the audience participates and "sees" them as well. This seems to explain many of the asides in the text. Abrupt transitions, often using "Behold," make the vision immediate to both the performer and the audience (e.g., 16:15).

4. I hear more clearly the call for congregations (plural) to listen to the Spirit (e.g., 2:7) as a sign that more than one congregation is expected to be present at a hearing of the text. The promises given after this call make clear that the advantages offered are to all congregations, not simply the one addressed in Jesus' "letter." This multicongregational gathering is also clear in 2:23 ("and all the congregations will know . . ."), which I perform by turning my attention throughout the room. This explains the plural "you" as addressing all seven congregations in the phrase "and I will give to you [plural] each according to your works." Elsewhere in the letter to Thyatira (2:18–28), the congregation is addressed with a singular "you" (e.g., "your [singular] deeds," in 2:19).

5. I hear more clearly the use of explanatory phrases throughout the text. In many cases, the Greek word *kai* is translated into English as "and," but would be better translated "that is," explaining the previous phrase. For example, Rev 1:2 is usually translated as "who testified to the word of God *and* to the testimony of Jesus." But the sense is that the "testimony of Jesus" is the word of God and John is trying to make sure the audience understands they are equivalents.[21] The verse is better performed as "who testified to the word of God, that is, the testimony of Jesus."

6. I have become more convinced about John's humble and self-effacing character, previously noted by scholars in the bumbling worship of angels (19:10; 22:9) and more tentatively in the interaction with the elder (7:13–14). To those three episodes, I add his self-identification as "brother" and "partner" (1:9), his weeping that no one is worthy to open the scroll (5:4), his misguided desire to write down the voice of the seven thunders (10:4), and his amazement by the Woman (17:6–7). In these passages he presents himself as no better than his audience, perhaps even worse! He is clueless, overly impressed by the immediate interpreters (i.e., angels and prophets like himself) and by the Woman Babylon. He is eager to know God's will but unworthy himself. He fails to worship God alone. John, just as much as his audience, needs to "see" and "hear" in order to "come out" of Babylon (18:4) and appropriately worship God.

7. I have become more attuned to the Seer's concern about creation. The visions pay attention to drinkable water, grass, trees, green things, and sea creatures. For example, John reveals anxiety over drinkable water. There is a threat that water will be contaminated by wormwood or blood (8:8, 11; 16:3–4), but a promise that "no one will thirst" in the New Jerusalem (7:16; 21:6; 22:17).[22] An example of John's personal interest in the health of creation is in the exclamation "the things

21. See also Rev 1:9; 6:9; 20:4. For discussion of epexegetical *kai*'s, see Blount, *Revelation*, 28.

22. For more on the ecological concerns of Revelation, see Barbara Rossing, "River of Life in God's New Jerusalem: An Ecological Vision for Earth's Future," *Mission Studies* 16 (January 1999): 136–56.

having lives" (8:9), which emphasizes that the sea creatures killed after the second trumpet plague are God's creatures, too. John elsewhere uses the word *life* (Greek, *psychē*) to describe human beings: the souls under the altar (6:9), believers who give their lives (12:11), slaves who are traded by Rome (18:3), and those who were beheaded because of their faith (20:4). John is concerned about life, not just human life, but the life of creatures, even in the chaotic sea. There is a complex embracing of all life in Revelation, yet willingness to give up life for the sake of faithfulness and endurance for God. I would not have come to this observation without having to perform Revelation.

8. Performing the Apocalypse has also heightened my sense of digressions in the text. As mentioned earlier, Revelation 7 is an example of a "digression," a departure from the logical sequence of a text. In performance, Rev 7:1 feels very natural following the passionate question, "Who is able to stand?" (6:17). When performing the question, I am hunched down with my hands up as if shielding myself from the wrath of God and the Lamb. Before Rev 7:1, I slowly stand and emphasize the four angels who are standing at the corners of the earth. The change in posture effects the transition with the stitch-word *stand*, both providing continuity from the previous vision and establishing a break between the results of the sixth seal and the restraint, delay, and sealing of Rev 7:1–8. The length of chapter 7 takes the performer and audience far afield from the scroll and seals, and, as many commentators have noted, brings them closer to the hymns of chapter 5. I emphasize this in 7:1 by walking from the position closer to the "Dragon" to the position closer to the heavenly throne (depending on the space available, it is only a few steps or as much as two meters).[23]

The digression is most notably felt by the performer in the transition from Rev 7:17 to 8:1, which abruptly returns to the formula used by the other six seals, "When the lamb opened. . . ." I try to reduce the audience's effort in understanding this transition by walking from the

23. Due to the constraints of the room, I chose not to have these two positions when I performed in November 2006. In retrospect, it may have been helpful to have retained some of my blocking even in the small space.

heavenly throne position toward the Dragon position. Some audience members responded that they did not feel the digressions as they thought they might. I was not surprised by this, as it is an unarticulated digression, meaning John does not explicitly say, "This was a digression."[24] An effective digression operates most of all on the emotional level rather than an intellectual level. As a digression, chapter 7 works to build the confidence of the hearers in God in order to endure and resist public pressure (and to endure the rest of the book!). Close study of the text reveals how the digression works, but to the audience the effect is primarily emotional.

9. On the subject of emotions, performing Revelation has emphasized to me how emotional the book is. It is exhausting to perform, oscillating between different voices, using extreme volume and gestures and emotions. The performer (through the voice of the glorified Jesus) shames and exhorts the audience directly in chapters 2–3. The remainder of the text oscillates between fear and confidence, with occasional anger and a few blessed moments of comic relief.

10. Finally, performance has helped me to detect hints of the John's weariness of the trials and plagues on the earth. For example, when I perform the introduction to the seven bowl plagues, "Then I saw another sign in heaven, great and amazing: seven angels who had the seven plagues, the last ones" (15:1), the phrase "the last one," comes out with relief that it is almost over. As I have suggested above, John is saddened and wearied by these events. He is at times gleeful at the way enemies suffer, but these events are a burden to him—and that burden is unavoidably passed on to the audience. When I say, "the last ones," I could see gratitude and relief in the audience's eyes, too. They also are ready to hear about the end of plagues and the beginning of healing.

24. See the discussion of articulated and unarticulated digressions as well as examples in Perry, *Rhetoric of Digressions*, 150–52.

5

Ten Insights from Performance Criticism

By preparing, internalizing, and performing texts, I have been given many insights into the texts themselves, the impact they have on audiences, and how biblical studies can change to better address how traditions were transmitted in ancient times and how they function in modern times. Of the many insights that could be chosen, here are my top ten.

1. Media Matters for Meaning

While it is too strong to say that "the medium is the message," the medium matters. Whether one is communicating face to face or via letter or inscription, the medium enables some possibilities while restricting others. A particular medium is enmeshed in a culture (i.e., values, attitudes, and behaviors) and within relationships of power.

For face-to-face communication, sound makes a difference to meaning. The tone of voice, pacing, volume, rhyming, and other features of the voice open up possibilities for the effects on an audience. A performer of Revelation can say, "Fallen, fallen is Babylon the Great" (Rev 18:1), in many ways. It can be said as a news reporter in matter-of-fact tones, as if "This just in: Fallen, fallen, is Babylon the Great." The audience is just receiving information. Or, the performer can say it with shock, as if they can't believe it has happened. She goes on to say, "It has happened!" as if "It really happened—can you believe it?" This interpretation may fit the responses of the kings, merchants, and shipmasters later in the chapter. Or the performer can say it with relief, responding to the violence of Babylon described earlier in Revelation 17 with thanks that it is over. The sound of the words shapes the effect on the audience.

It is not enough to say that sound matters to meaning. Face-to-face communication also has the possibilities of gestures, facial expressions, and movements that can augment the voice with other signs. Gestures to the audience to "come out of Babylon" (Rev 18:4) make the command personal to the people gathered in that occasion, while simply reading the text (even with intonation) will not have the same impact.

Face-to-face communication is limited by the extent to which a performance or audience can remember information. I've noted in the examples of performing Habakkuk and Revelation that most audiences experience the emotions of the performance but are able to remember only a few ideas. Ideas linked with strong emotions are easier for them to recall; fear especially seems stronger than confidence. Repetition increases what an audience will remember. For example, audiences seem to remember the phrase "repent" from Revelation 1–3 more easily than the One-Sitting-On-the-Throne saying, "Behold! I am making all things new" (21:5). Even by emphasizing this line by tone and pacing, an audience can't easily recall that this is one of only two times that God speaks, making this a significant line.

Handwritten media (such as letters and manuscripts) have the advantage of repeated access to precise words and the opportunity for detailed study. These media, however, are limited by a number of factors. In the ancient world, only a small number of people had the ability to read fluently. Reading often was in service to elites. Thus writing and reading were enmeshed in power relations that could have an impact on meaning, especially when the writing was performed for an audience. For example, when Luke presents Jesus as a kind of scribe in Luke 4, he is appealing to a scribal culture that values someone who has been educated to handle and read a scroll fluently. Jesus' authority, in Luke's telling of the story, is similar to the authority of scribes who could read and whose audience's yielded them power. In contrast, Mark portrays Jesus as having a different kind of authority than the scribes. "They were astounded at his teaching, for he taught them as one having authority, and not as the scribes" (Mark 1:22). In other words, for some audiences being able to read fluently was a sign of authority, while for other audiences scribal identity was to be rejected in favor of face-to-face communication skills.

Handwritten media are also limited by having only the visual signs of the letters and not features of the voice or body to clarify the communicator's intent. The performer, audience, and situation can either amplify or resist the effects the text may suggest. Paul expects his letter to the Thessalonians to be read aloud to all the believers (1 Thess 5:27). How will the reader say, "Now concerning the times and the seasons, brothers and sisters, you do not need to have anything written to you" (5:1)? Will she perform it in a tone of chastising, as if to say, "You should know better!" Or will she have seen the word *encourage* in 5:11, and say this line with more encouragement, like a cheerleader? Or will she have read the whole letter in a flat tone that put everyone to sleep? The embodiment by the performer and the specific state of the audience will have dramatic impact on the meaning.

Written media are also subject to change by new performers with new audiences and situations. Awareness of this limitation led John to put a warning against changes to the text at the end of Revelation (22:18–19). The text is now autonomous of the author. For example, as may have happened in Qumran, a performer may choose not to perform the psalm of Habakkuk 3. The effect may be to dwell on the lament to God about the persecution of the Righteous One and the injustice of the Man, the Babylonian king. God's coming justice is proclaimed (chapter 2), but without the concluding tension between praise of God's victory and resignation to the coming invasion.

Performance criticism illuminates the dynamics of media cultures for those who are studying the Bible. The media makes a difference in meaning.

2. Performance Opens Some Interpretations and Closes Others

In the process of preparing, internalizing, and performing a text, some interpretations of the text are revealed while others are eliminated. For example, it was only in performing Habakkuk that it seemed possible to read the prophet interrupting God in Hab 1:6. God reveals, "For behold, I am raising the Chaldeans!," and the prophet interrupts:

> That hurtful and hasty nation?
> the Man who marches across expanses of the earth
> to take possession of dwelling places that are not his own?

This possibility emerged after many attempts to make God's voice consistent within and between chapters 1 and 2.

In other instances, an interpretation may be eliminated. On the surface, one could read that Jesus is asking questions of his disciples and expects a response. "Why are you talking about having no bread? Do you still not perceive or understand? Are your hearts hardened? Do you have eyes, and fail to see? Do you have ears, and fail to hear? And do you not remember?" (Mark 8:17–18). Even in the most flat, emotionless reading, however, it becomes apparent that these are rhetorical questions. Jesus is expressing frustration.

Performance criticism offers students and scholars of the Bible a new way to explore and compare interpretations of a text.

3. Biblical Texts Are a Whole-Body Experience

Whenever a text is read aloud to a person or a group of people, it is an embodied performance. It is a whole-body experience for performer and audience, even if the performer does not move their eyes off a page or hands off a podium. The person moves to a position to read and assumes a posture (sitting or standing). The person moves away from the reading position. More than likely, even a minimally fluent performance will involve some gestures of head and hand.

The performance of a text will have increased impact when the performer appropriately uses the advantages of face-to-face communication, which include intonation, pacing, volume, gestures, facial expressions, and movement. The word *appropriate* is the key. What is appropriate for the particular audience and situation to reach the desired effects? In ancient Greece and Rome, rhetoricians such as Quintilian taught appropriate gestures. Others did not think that orators should be too dramatic, lest audiences not take the speaker seriously. The key point is that performers embodied texts in ways to lower the audience's efforts to reach desired effects.

Performance criticism helps readers of the Bible reconnect the body (including emotions) with the mind in experiencing the text.

4. Meaning Made in Community

Since the Enlightenment, some readers have thought that meaning was produced when an individual mentally processed words on a page. In the twentieth century, we have rediscovered that meaning-making is more accurately understood as participatory. We interpret experiences in community. Performance criticism extends this insight to show that meaning (or "effect") is made by performance in community. To use the technical way of saying this, performance is a participatory way of knowing (an "epistemology"), not an individualized one.[1]

Performances of biblical texts are attempts to reinforce or modify the culture of a group of people, have an impact on power relations, and shape identity. We have seen how this works on many levels. For example, John re-performs other prophetic phrases and passages, such as example from Daniel and Zechariah. He uses their words and the audience's familiarity to construct a prophetic identity and to persuade

1. Dwight Conquergood, "Performance Studies: Interventions and Radical Research," *The Drama Review* 46, no. 2 (Summer 2002): 149.

them to yield him power and influence. He shares his visions, using these prior prophetic performances to modify their culture. He wants to persuade them to give up a comfortable lifestyle of trade within the Roman imperial system. In order to do that, in performance he helps them envision a new identity: followers of the slaughtered Lamb, willing to be slaughtered in witness and resistance.

This analysis, which conforms to what many scholars have concluded, is not necessarily what the audiences of my performances have experienced. As much as I (and other scholars) would like to believe we have power over how audiences understand these texts, the meaning-making is participatory and communal. Like other scholarly performers, I subtly and explicitly try to persuade audiences to yield power to me. But as the surveys described in chapter 4 have shown, audiences bring their own preconceptions and are more affected by emotions raised in performance and not necessarily by ideas.

Performance criticism humbles biblical studies to realize that meaning-making is participatory and done in community, not by expert individuals.

5. Myriad Performances Mean Variation without an "Original" Version

Performance criticism also exposes the unreality of a search for an "original" version. Even if we assume that a manuscript has all the words and letters that an author penned, we can't reproduce the embodiment that the author envisioned. Even if the exact words are used in the same language, every performer of that text will say the words slightly differently based on their own preferences and interpretation. Every audience will hear it differently based on their preconceptions and the situation.

To make it concrete, consider the way Eusebius describes the Gospel of Mark in his *Ecclesiastical History*. If Mark indeed had been a scribe to Peter and had listened to Peter preach and tell the story of Jesus hundreds (or thousands?) of times before writing episodes in his notebook and finally assembling them into his Gospel, then which is the "original"? The first time Peter preached? The way Mark wrote the episodes in his book? The first version that assembled episodes? The whole notion of an "original" becomes silly. We don't have access to any of these "firsts," and all we can say is that there were many performances of similar material.

When we make the picture more complex by admitting that scribes altered manuscripts to fit their performance, it becomes even harder to speak of an original. Isn't it "original" for that scribe with that audience and in that situation? It is far more useful to compare different manuscripts as different performances of the same material.

Performance criticism, in this way, offers a more accurate and fruitful way to think about the production of the texts we have. We abandon the search for an authoritative "original" (which is often an attempt at intervening in contemporary culture and power relations), and instead compare performances of similar material, whether in ancient manuscripts, literary and archeological evidence, or in modern performances.

6. Memory Is the Essential Context for Performer, Audience, and Interpreter

One of the rediscoveries of the twentieth century was the role of memory in transmitting and influencing biblical traditions. This paralleled the growing awareness of how memory works in human communication.

Memory is the essential context for understanding the Bible. Biblical traditions and stories existed, therefore, in memory before writing. Parents taught children proverbs, laws, and identity-shaping stories, having them repeat them and embody them in performances. Prophets and evangelists told their memories of visionary experiences and encounters with the divine in human history. People who heard these proverbs, laws, and stories read from written texts would compare them to their memories, and react to changes of which they were aware. They might vocally criticize a version that didn't fit their memory, or laugh at a performance that spoofed a previous version.

No text, therefore, can be read without acknowledgment of the memories that the reader brings to it. It is helpful to survey an audience's preconceived notions (i.e., memories) before a performance in order to better assess the impact a performance has had on them.

Because memory is the essential context, it is worth the time and effort of a biblical scholar to internalize a text. The repetition involved in internalization is the best way to understand what assumptions a text has on a person's memory. For example, my difficulty in remembering small interruptions to Revelation, such as the eagle's woes in Rev 8:13, highlights their importance. They slow the pace and draw attention to the attempt to separate the audience from "those dwelling on earth."

Performance criticism draws attention to the dynamics of memory as the context for performer, audience, and interpretation.

7. Genres Blur and Influence Each Other

It is traditional in biblical studies to isolate genres (oratory, poetry, prose, drama, history, biography). For example, we make clear that oratory carries an assumption that the speaker has a clear purpose and a certain style in performance. Poetry is more evocative than clear, and may rhyme or have other stylistic features. Some ancient orators and philosophers wanted to keep the boundaries clear between oratory, poetry, and drama.

Performance criticism shows how the boundaries between genres are more fluid. Habakkuk blends prophetic lament with visionary experiences and psalms. Revelation merges the genres of letter and prophecy. Examples could be given from Aristotle (one of those who insists on genre distinctions), who cites dramatic works in his discussion of oratory and compares favorably emotions generated in oratory with those evoked in drama.

While it is helpful to describe the assumptions an audience may have based on their memories of a particular genre, it is inaccurate to assume there are rigid boundaries between them. Orators used dramatic techniques. Dramas included scenes with orators speaking.

Biblical performers also blurred the boundaries between history, prophecy, psalm, letter, and other genres.

Performance criticism gives insight into the ways audience's expectations of genre play a role in how a text is received.

8. Biblical Writers Are Enmeshed Participants Rather Than Objective Observers

Perhaps as a result of the Enlightenment, some would like the biblical authors to be objective observers writing only what they see and hear. This suggests their reliability and authority. It also reveals that this assertion is one way to perform the Bible in order to shape culture, power relations, and identity.

Biblical writers are storytellers, however. They were active participants in communities who were making meaning of the events they experienced. They told the stories in a way that made sense to them and their audiences. They chose words and memories that fit the situation in which they found themselves. In other words, they were enmeshed participants and not at all objective.

For some, this is a disheartening loss of reliability and authority. For some, it evokes grief over loss of faith. If we can't count on the Bible as objective fact of "what happened," then what?

Performance criticism offers another way to think about this change in perspective. People who told and wrote biblical stories and traditions internalized them and were shaped by them. Likewise, they used these stories to shape the culture, power relations, and identity of their community. In a similar way, modern people are invited to internalize the text and struggle with the text's culture, power relations, and identity. Such struggle leads to people today becoming enmeshed performers of living traditions rather than objective observers of ancient and dead ones.

9. Performance Is Inevitably Both Conservative and Innovative

A text is a part of a living tradition when it is performed in community.

The community yields power to those who conserve the tradition. For example, scribes in Jesus' day were educated in preserving, copying, performing, and interpreting the scrolls. The community also holds performers accountable to the memory of the tradition. These power relations help to conserve the tradition.

There are also communal pressures to innovate the tradition. As social, economic, or political changes alter the situation, performances will naturally be heard in new ways and performed in new ways. In chapters 3 and 4, I discussed how Habakkuk and Revelation were heard in the *world in front of the text.* The Teacher of Righteousness, the leader of the Qumran community, became identified with the "Righteous One" of Habakkuk. For Paul, the "Righteous One" was the believer who lived by faith. Innovation arises as the performer and audience hear a living tradition in a new situation.

Performance criticism gives insights into the conservation and innovation of traditions in both ancient and modern communities.

10. Performance Reunites the Pieces Fragmented by Critical Biblical Scholarship

When I had finished my doctoral program and was preparing to leave Chicago, I asked one of my professors what he thought biblical studies needed. He said, "Unity. Biblical studies is more fragmented than ever before, with everyone using their own methods. It's harder and harder for biblical scholars to talk with each other!"

Performance criticism offers a way toward reuniting biblical studies as a discipline. First, in method and practice, performance criticism embraces the insights of every kind of biblical scholarship from the historical-critical method to narrative criticism to postcolonial criticism. It is not necessary to be a specialist in every discipline, but performance criticism gives a framework for each discipline to be valued and brought into conversation.

Second, the performance itself offers a way to reintegrate the insights of scholarship into a seamless whole. Critical methods are inevitably reductive: they break the text, the author, the performer, the audience, the situation down into smaller and smaller pieces to understand them in detail. It is the same move made in the hard sciences, as scientists break down a substance into smaller and smaller parts, from the ore to the element to the atom to the subatomic level. All that's left after the analysis is subatomic pieces that seem useless to anyone outside the discipline. In the same way, biblical studies can break down a text such as Revelation into analysis of Greek words, social situation, feminist critique, liberation analysis, dispensational theories, and an unlimited number of pieces. But none of these disciplines is able to put them back into a whole that a nonspecialist can understand.

Performance does this. When scholars becomes performers, they integrate all the fruits of their inquiry into their performance for an audience. They are attentive to all the nuances and how they will communicate the tiniest details through their voice, word choice, movement, facial expressions, gestures, and so on. The audience doesn't need any special training. The performance brings it all together.

Performance criticism doesn't mean we need fewer scholarly disciplines. Performance criticism shows us we need more performers—scholars, pastors, and students who have done the hard work of breaking down a text to understand its most minute details and are willing put it back together again in a performance.

6

Conclusions, Challenges, and Considerations

They are performers with texts and audiences in concrete situations. The father sits with his son practicing commandments. The reader opens the book and occasionally looks up at the group as she reads. The storyteller sits with others in a circle sharing a well-known tale. The leader reminds the group of their founder's words and draws out new implications for their situation. The scribe explains what the law means for the people assembled. The song leader guides the rehearsal of a choir. The group follows the script of the annual gathering. A scholar reads her paper that analyzes the nuances of a single word. In each case, there is a *performer* (or performers), a *text*, an *audience*, and a *situation*.

Biblical performance criticism takes each event as an opportunity for study. Anytime a passage found in the Bible (no matter how short or long) is read out loud for an audience (one or more people), it is a performance event for analysis. In some cases the "text" exists only in memory. That is, the performer shares a tradition that may not yet have been written but will be written in some form in the future. Stories about Jesus healing a leper out in the countryside were told first by eyewitnesses who heard the man himself proclaiming it, then secondary witnesses, and so on. Each time, something changed: a new performer or a new audience or a new situation that changed the way the story was heard, even if only in impact. The story circulated before it was written down by someone we call "Mark." Eyewitnesses could have heard it performed and corrected the storyteller publicly or privately. It was performed after Mark wrote a version he heard and told. We refer to these kind of stories as "texts" because we have access only through writings that have been performed and re-performed—read, copied, and transmitted through the years. We now refer to "Mark 1:40–45" to find the story quickly in the collection we call "the Bible" so we may perform the story anew. But each text represents many performances. Thousands? Millions? Tens of millions, perhaps even billions now, of performers, audiences, and situations before and after the text was written. There are worlds of performance behind the text, in front of the text, and even in the world created by the text in the imagination. Each performance event is an object for inquiry, imagination, and intervention. As a way of understanding the Bible, performance criticism accounts for how we understand human communication to work in general and how traditions are transmitted and used in communities that value them.

Performance as intervention means getting involved. Critical study of the Bible no longer can claim objectivity. To study is to perform, to intervene in the values, behavior, and attitudes of real people in a culture, people in real power relations, whose identities are shaped by the performances in which they participate. To become a performance critic is to become a performer.

Intervention brings the fruits of inquiry and imagination to our situation and our communities. How can we listen to the prophets' cry for justice without seeing the need for justice for exploited workers at garment factories in Sri Lanka, just for one example? How can we hear John's grief over the death of "living creatures" in the sea without grieving and acting on the overfishing of Chilean sea bass or the destruction of habitat of the tiny bala shark? How can we hear Jesus say he brings good news to the poor without being concerned about the vulnerable in our time and place? Internalizing these voices makes it impossible to ignore them.

Our performances make a difference for better or worse and for health or sickness. Some have performed biblical texts as part of a strategy to keep people enslaved. Others have used passages to keep women silent. Others quote, "The poor will always be with you," as a reason to ignore the needs of the hungry. Performances are always interventions.

The way to counter performances of the Bible that are destructive is with more effective and persuasive performances. We become more effective communicators when we have prepared, internalized, and performed biblical traditions. I take the essential message of the Hebrew Bible and the New Testament to be that the God of life and hope overcomes death and despair. This message is most effective when it is embodied. Biblical performance criticism, as it embraces intervention, trains scholars to be effective performers who have an impact on culture, power relations, and identity for the health and life of others, especially those who are most vulnerable and voiceless.

Challenges and Considerations for the Future

Biblical performance criticism is still emerging as a discipline. My presentation in this book is my synthesis of scholarship and performance to this point. I would be claiming too much to say that all performance critics would agree with every aspect of my presentation. My work is dependent on many people's work, but in this particular presentation it is wholly my own. In a similar way, Luke's Gospel is wholly his own even as it is a synthesis of Mark and other sources, that is, other performers of stories about Jesus. This book is not the last performance on performance criticism!

At least five particular challenges face this emerging discipline: (1) more specific descriptions of ancient performances; (2) clarifying the relationship between ancient and modern performances; (3) developing better survey skills and tools to assess audience impact;

(4) listening closely across cultures; and (5) persuading scholars to perform.

First, we need more *specific descriptions of ancient performances*. Early in the development of performance criticism, we were too absolute in some claims. We said almost every text was memorized and that the scroll or codex wouldn't be looked at. We implied every text would have been emotionally presented. We insisted that texts were rarely read individually and in private. We made a sharp distinction between the written and oral media (called "the Great Divide"). We used to say things like, "only 10 percent of people around the Mediterranean could read." At the time, these generalizations were helpful to draw attention to the neglected importance of oral communication in the ancient world (I suggest "face-to-face communication" to incorporate the body's role). The time for these generalizations is over.[1]

The time for specific descriptions of ancient performances is here. Performance critics need to be more careful and specific about performance scenarios in the ancient world. For example, important work has been done by William Johnson, Holt Parker, and Robert Bagnall on differences between Roman and Greek writing culture and the range of everyday writing in the first century CE.[2] I have deliberately avoided using the word *literacy* or referring to a percentage of people who could "read" because the very concept of "literacy" requires nuance and data for each different time and place.[3] It is better to discuss specific pieces of evidence from performances. For example, the Greek orator Dio of Prusa is a relevant source for

1. Werner Kelber, who used the so-called Great Divide between orality and literacy to promote understanding the Bible as functioning in primarily oral cultures, was also among the first to deconstruct it. For example, see Werner H. Kelber, "Words and Tradition: Words in Time, Words in Space," in *Semeia 65: Orality and Textuality in Early Christian Literature*, ed. Joanna Dewey (Atlanta: Scholars Press, 1995), 139–67. See the responses in the same volume by John Miles Foley, "Words in Tradition, Words in Text: A Response," 169–80; and Bernard Brandon Scott, "Blowing in the Wind: A Response," 181–91.
2. William A. Johnson and Holt N. Parker, *Ancient Literacies: The Culture of Reading in Greece and Rome* (New York: Oxford University Press, 2011); William Allen Johnson, *Readers and Reading Culture in the High Roman Empire: A Study of Elite Communities* (New York: Oxford University Press, 2010); Roger S. Bagnall, *Everyday Writing in the Græco-Roman East* (Berkeley: University of California Press, 2012).
3. Although brief, one of the best discussions of "literacy" is Lucretia B. Yaghjian, "Ancient Reading," in *The Social Sciences and New Testament Interpretation*, ed. Richard Rohrbaugh (Peabody, MA: Hendrickson, 1996), 206–30.

performances in Asia Minor in the late first century CE that may be fruitfully compared with performances of Revelation, 1 Peter, Galatians, and other works performed in Greek in that time and location.

Second, the *relationship between a modern performance and an ancient performance* needs to be clarified. What can be learned about ancient performances by performing a text today? Some have argued that all we can say is that we gained some insight into the text that helped us go back and inquire into the historical situation differently. We might call this a "heuristic" use of modern performances (from the Greek word for "find" or "discover"). A modern performance helps us discover insights that other critical methods help to verify.

I have suggested that we can go farther. With a general theory of human communication, we can draw parallels to how performers and audiences communicate. With culturally sensitive descriptions of emotions and gestures, we can compare means of persuading people. With appropriate comparisons, we may be able to better suggest that a modern audience's response may mirror or at least correlate to an ancient audience's response. I have offered here only beginning points for further development.

Third, performance critics need better *training and tools to assess the effects of performance on audiences.* This is a crucial part of performance criticism, to assess intervention and complete the loop from intervention back to inquiry. In chapters 3 and 4, I used surveys to quantitatively assess what impact my performances of Habakkuk and Revelation had on the audiences. The surveys showed that the audiences were changed by the performance. But I also was able to show that my desired effects were not always achieved. I provided evidence that audiences don't always hear what scholars hear. But I have no training to develop surveys, only questions that seem to get at the desired effects of a performance.

Performance criticism will need to integrate more practices and insights from ethnography and survey methodology. Ethnography is the study of people and culture. Sessions of the Bible and Ancient and

Modern Media (BAMM) group at the 2014 and 2015 Annual Meetings of the Society of Biblical Literature were dedicated to the work of sociologist Gary Alan Fine on reputation-making as applied to ancient performances. More could be done with ethnographic methods on assessing modern performances. Survey methodology widely used in social sciences could also help to assess how modern audiences experience performances and perhaps shed light on the dynamics of ancient performances.

Fourth, performance critics need to *listen closely across cultures.* Specifically, we need to be open to criticism when we universalize insights rather than being sensitive to the particular cultural situation. At its best, performance criticism offers a method and practice to become more sensitive to the cultural situations of both performer and audience.[4] At their worst, performance critics may ask audiences' to yield power to the "experts" and their construction of how biblical texts "should" be performed.

For example, Nathan Esala recognizes the methodological advantages of biblical performance criticism, but warns that it was developed in a North American context to serve particular interests. As he works in Ghana with the Bikɔɔm, he observes that performance criticism will need to be recontextualized. "I recognize that many Bikɔɔm church leaders have resisted Bible engagement strategies that they perceive as exclusively oral, strategies that effectively isolate and marginalize them in a pre-modern, non-progressive state."[5] Not everyone will receive a dramatic performance as "Bible," and in fact, they may reject it as a continuation of colonial condescension. The challenge is for performance critics to be sensitive to the power relations involved in practicing this new discipline.

Fifth, performers need to *persuade scholars to perform.* The payoff for performing is a deeper understanding of the text, an integration of all

4. For example, see James A. Maxey, *From Orality to Orality: A New Paradigm for Contextual Translation of the Bible* (Eugene, OR: Cascade, 2009).

5. Nathan Esala, "Ideology and Bible Translation: Can Biblical Performance Criticism Help?," *The Bible Translator* 66, no. 3 (2015): 216–29, at 217.

that has been learned, and an opening of one's mind as to what matters and what doesn't matter for an audience hearing the text.

Margaret Lee had studied the sound of the Greek of the Sermon on the Mount, but had never performed it herself.[6] She cherished the rhythm and rhyme of the Sermon in Greek when she studied it silently, but when she had to translate it into English to perform, she recognized the difficulties. She wrote, "How to communicate related concepts that Sermon associates through rhythm and rhyme, when the words for their English equivalents diverge and clash? How to convey the Sermon's many switches back and forth between the second person singular and plural? I became uneasy with the compromises I found necessary." She had studied the sound of each Greek syllable, but when she had to perform the Sermon she had to face the coherence of the whole work for her audience.

> My sustained, microscopic analysis of the Sermon's sounds had neglected the Sermon's coherence as a literary whole, and the transitions from one section to the next. Although I felt confident that I understood each of the Sermon's parts, I felt at a loss as I tried to capture the overall mood of the Sermon. Is it placid, angry, frustrated, patient, variable? Are the beatitudes consoling or sarcastic? How should the Lord's Prayer sound in the middle? Is the prohibition of anxiety reassuring or testy? Is there any other way to end the Sermon than by shouting? And how does the Sermon's emotional tone modulate from one section to the next?

Performing the Sermon on the Mount opened new questions and issues that she had never considered, even with her close and detailed study.

In short, it is worth the time of every student and scholar of the Bible to perform. How can we ask the right questions of a text unless we get inside the primary way it is communicated? How can we reunite the text that has been broken down into its smallest parts? The process of preparing, internalizing, and performing a text allows us inside the communication of these traditions and unites the insights of many

6. The following quotations are taken from Margaret E. Lee, "My First Experience Performing," http://www.biblicalperformancecriticism.org/index.php/10-news/performance-reflections/101-my-first-experience-performing.

disciplines. Performance criticism offers an exciting future for biblical studies and those who perform biblical traditions every week.

Appendix A: A Translation of Habakkuk for Performance

Prepared for performance by Peter S. Perry. Based on a translation by Jeanette Mathews, *Performing Habakkuk: Faithful Re-enactment in the Midst of Crisis* (Eugene, OR: Pickwick, 2012; used by permission of Wipf and Stock Publishers). With insights from *Tanakh: The Holy Scriptures* (Philadelphia: Jewish Publication Society, 1985), abbreviated JPS.

Parentheses ( ) indicate a significant translation decision, including the addition of word(s) not in the Hebrew.

Gestures and rhetorical notes are made in the callout boxes.

[*Hold up closed scroll and unroll. Place on stand.*]
1:1 (This is) the revelation that Habakkuk the
prophet saw.

The Prophet to the L*ORD:*
[*Looking up with hands out and upwards, plaintive and frustrated.*]
2 How long, LORD,
all I call and you not hear?
I cry out to you, 'violence!' and you do not save?

3 Why do you make me look at sorrow [*Gesture to places beyond audience*]
and pay attention to trouble? — *Gesture: hands from eyes to imagined trouble.*

Devastation and violence are before me — *Gesture: hands up to face.*
And there is strife! And contention carries on.
Gesture upwards.

4 As a result, (your Instruction) is paralyzed
and justice never goes forth. — *Gesture: Hands from body going out towards audience.*

For wickedness surrounds the righteous person,
So crooked justice goes forth.

Emphasize crooked in contrast with previous "justice." Gesture crookedly from body.

The Lord *to the audience:*

Step to left side "God's position" and look down at audience. Deeper voice. Gesture and look directly at audience.

5 All of you, look at the nations and pay attention!
And be profoundly astounded!
For a work is being worked in your days
—you wouldn't believe it if it was retold!

With confident tone that God is answering Habakkuk's complaint.

6 For behold, I am raising the Chaldeans!

The surprise: God is behind the rise of the Babylonian Empire.

The Prophet to the Lord:
That hurtful and hasty nation?
the Man who marches across expanses of the earth

Quickly step back to "prophet position" and look up at God, waving hands and interrupting.

to take possession of dwelling places
that are not his own?
7 He is terrible and fearful,

Pointing to stage left to spatialize and personify Babylonian king.

Hands marching from right to left, grabbing as going.

From him, his justice and his dignity
go forth.

Pointing to "Man" position (right) with astonishment.

8 And swifter than leopards are his horses
and keener than the wolves of the evening.
And they gallop, his gallopers and
his gallopers!
From far they come, they fly!
Like a vulture, he hastens to eat.

Sarcastic emphasis on "his" to distinguish from God's justice, dignity. "Go forth" gesture repeated from 1:4.

9 Every one comes for violence.
The eagerness of their faces shows,
And he gathered captives like sand.
10 And as for him, at the kings he scoffs
and rulers are a (joke) to him!

Pointing to "Man" position (right).

As for him, at every fortress he laughs!
And he (mounded dirt) and captured them.

Make mound gesture that will connect with 2:1 "siege mound."

11 Then, he swept through like the wind
and he passed by and was guilty,
(for he gives credit to his god for his strength).[1]

(Pause, shaking head)

12 Aren't you everlasting, LORD?
My God of holiness, you never die!

With shock—God would choose the King of Babylon as justice for Jerusalem's injustice?! Gesturing to "Man" position.

LORD, for justice you set him?
My Rock, for rebuke you established him?

Repeat "pay attention" gesture from 1:3.

13 Your eyes are too pure to look at evil!
And you are not able to pay attention
to trouble!

Open handed "Why?"

Why do you pay attention to those who act treacherously?
(Why do) you keep silence when wickedness swallows the
righteous person?

14 You made humankind like the fish of the sea,
like a lowly sea-creature with no-one
ruling over it.

Pointing at the Man (the King of Babylon).

Gesture: like fishing rod.

15 Every one he brought up with a fishing hook,
he drags away with his net,

Gesture: dragging net.

and gathers him with his fish-trap.

Gesture: encircling.

So, he is glad and rejoices!

Gesture: pointing to "Man" position.

16 Therefore, he sacrifices to his net
And offers smoke to his fish-trap!
For with them, his portion grew rich
And his food was fat.

17 Shall he therefore empty his net and continue
to slay nations without mercy?

The Prophet to the audience:

Pause and slow: asking audience permission.

2:1 On my guard let me stand,
and let me set myself on a siege mound,
and let me keep watch to see what the LORD says to me,
and what I will bring back concerning my rebuke.

1. Following JPS.

(Pause, listening)

2 And the LORD did answer me and said,

Step left and look down from "God position." Deeper voice.

The LORD to the prophet:

Write (the) vision and make (it) plain on the tablets
So that (the) reader will run with it.
3 For (the) vision is still for the appointed time,
and it testifies[2] to the end and does not lie.
If it tarries, wait for it! For it surely comes; it will not delay.

The LORD to the audience:

Pointing to "Man position."

4 Behold, he is puffed up;[3] his soul is not right within him,
but the righteous person in faithfulness will live.
5 Moreover, (wealth deceives)![4]

Holding finger up to wait: there is more!

A mighty man is arrogant and won't last,
One who widens his soul like a grave,
So, he is like death and never satisfied.
And he gathered to himself all the nations,
And collected to himself all the peoples.
6 Aren't all these people and nations lifting a taunt against him?
(Aren't they composing) mocking riddles about him?
(The LORD) says,[5]

Nodding head as if the assuming the audience agrees with the general principle of justice and its application to the Man.

Woe to the one who piles up what is not his
—how (much longer)?[6]
And the one making himself rich with loans!

2. Mathews, *Performing Habakkuk*, 217, with Roberts and Anderson.

3. With JPS; see Mathews, *Performing Habakkuk*, 122.

4. See ibid., 124 n.4. This seems to fit the upcoming theme of "collecting" and "gathering" with the wealth decried by the first Woe.

5. Ibid., 128, 132, takes these Woes to be proclaimed by the Lord against the Babylonian king. The general (and sapiential) character of the woes suggests to me that they are more general—applying to both injustice in Israel as well as the injustice Babylon is bringing. By God announcing the Woes, there is a common standard of justice for all people.

6. Following the direction of JPS.

7 Will not your creditors suddenly arise
And will not the collectors for you wake?[7]
And you will be their spoil!

> *Turn to face "Man" position and directly address.*

8 Because you plundered many nations
let the remaining peoples plunder you
on account of human blood spilled and violence against
the land,
every village, and all who live in it.[8]

> *Turn back to audience for general wisdom statement.*

9 Woe to the one who violently gains unjust gain!
Evil belongs to his house
Who has set his nest in the heights
To be delivered from the grasp of evil.

> *Turn to face "Man" and directly address.*

10 You counseled shame for your house,
To cut off many people. "Your soul is sinning"

> *Gesture to wall and hand holding stone.*

11 A stone from a wall will cry out,
And a rafter from the woodwork will answer it.

> *Gesture to rafter in ceiling.*

12 Woe to the one who builds a city with
bloodshed
and establishes a village with iniquity,
so that people labor for fire and nations grow faint for nothing.[9]

> *Turn back to audience for general wisdom statement.*

Interjection:

> *Step back into "Prophet" position, with wonder.*

13 Behold, is it not from the LORD of hosts
14 that the earth will be filled
with the knowledge of the glory of the LORD
as the waters cover the sea!

> *Step back into "God position" and address audience with general wisdom statement.*

15 Woe to the one making his neighbors drink even to drunkenness
and pour out rage
in order to gave upon their nakedness![10]

---

7. See JPS and NASB.
8. Following NASB; see JPS.
9. With JPS, moving this phrase into v. 12.
10. With JPS.

16 You are satisfied with shame rather than glory.

Turn to directly address "the Man."

So, drink up and be counted among the uncircumcised![11]
A cup in the right hand of the LORD will turn around on you,

Hold imaginary cup in right hand.

And shameful shame will be on your glory.

Gesture cup spilling on "the Man."

17 For the violence of Lebanon covers you,
And the devastation of beasts causes them to be terrified
on account of human blood spilled and violence
against the land,
every village, and all who live in it.[12]

Turn to address audience with general wisdom statements.

18 Of what benefit is an idol when the one who carved it made it?[13]
—an image and a teacher of deception!
For the maker who makes it trusts it,
Making dumb, worthless idols!

Point to "the Man." Interestingly, there is no direct second-person address with this final woe.

19 Woe to the one who says to a tree, 'wake up!'
'awake!' to the mute stone. 'Shhh! It is teaching!'
Behold it, overlaid with gold and silver
And full of wind? There is nothing in it!

The Prophet to the audience:

Step back into "Prophet position."

20 But the LORD is in his temple of holiness
Hush before him, all the Earth!

3:1 A prayer of Habakkuk the prophet, to the tune of Shigionoth.

(Teach chanted refrain to congregation)
2 LORD, I have heard of your reputation,
I am in awe, LORD, of your work!

11. I take this as one of the clearest signs that these are general Woes, towards both Jews and non-Jews.

12. Matching 2:8, following NASB; see JPS. See Mathews, *Performing Habakkuk*, 132.

13. Following JPS.

(Chanted)
In the midst of years, you will make your | people live.
In the midst of years, you will make | yourself known.
In turmoil, you will remember | compassion
3 God comes from Teman
and (the) Holy One from | Mount Paran. *Selah.*
(refrain)

His splendor has clothed the | heavens
And his praise has | filled the earth.
4 And bright as the | light it is,
rays from his | hand has he.
And there is a hiding place | for his strength.
5 Before him, Pest- | ilence marches
and Firebolt goes forth be- | fore his feet.
6 He has taken his stand and he | measures earth.
He has looked and he makes | nations free.
And (he) has shattered the moun- | tains of old,
Bent down the | ancient hills.
The ways of | old are his.
7 Below I saw trouble at the | tents of Cushan
Let the pavilions[14] be in turmoil in the land of | Midian.
8 Has the LORD burned ag- | ainst the Rivers?
Is your face ag- | ainst the Rivers?
Is your fury ag- | ainst the Sea?
For you ride | on your horses,
On your chariots | of salvation.
9 Indeed laid bare is your bow,
sworn are the spears | of your word. *Selah.*
(Refrain)

With streams you | cleave the land.
10 Having looked at you, | mountains shake!

14. JPS.

A torrent of | rain comes down![15]
(The) Deep gives | up its voice!
Sun has lifted its | hands on high!
11 Moon has stood in its lo- | fty abode!
As light, your | arrows dart,
as brightness, your | glittering spear.
12 In indignation you stride | through the earth.
In anger you | tread down nations.
13 You go forth to | save your people,
to save your | anointed one.
You will smash the roof of the house of | wickedness,
to lay bare from found- | ation to top.[16] *Selah*

(Refrain)

Pointing to the Man.

14 You have pierced with his spears the head of | his warriors,
who stormed out to | scatter me.
They relish devouring the | poor in secret,[17]
15 but you have walked through the Sea (with) your horses,
a heap | of great waters.

The Prophet to the audience:

16 I heard and my belly is in turmoil,
at the voice my lips tingled.
Decay comes into my bones,
And in my place I am in turmoil,
where I wait for a day of distress
to come up to a people who will invade us.
17 If the fig tree does not sprout,
and no produce is on the vines,
if the yield of the olive tree has failed
and fields have not produced food,
the flock has been cut off from the fold
and no cattle are in the stalls,

15. JPS.
16. Following JPS; tying into the "house" theme of 2:9-11.
17. Following JPS.

18 yet I will exult in the LORD,
I will rejoice in the God of my salvation.
19 The LORD my Lord is my strength.
He places my feet like the hinds'
And on my high places he makes me walk.

To the Director, to the tune of Niginoth.

Appendix B: A Translation of Revelation 17–19 for Performance

Prepared for performance by Peter S. Perry.

Parentheses ( ) indicate a significant translation decision, including the addition of word(s) not in the Greek.

~~Strikethrough~~ indicates an omission of a Greek word in the translation.

Brackets [ ] indicate a text critical issue, as indicated in the 27th edition of the Nestle Aland *Novum Testamentum Graece* (Greek New Testament).

Gestures and performance notes are made in the callout boxes.

THE END OF BABYLON (17:1–19:10)

1. *The woman sitting on the beast (17:1-18)*

a) Introduction & Audition

Slow down, reduced intensity for ekphrasis.

17:1a Then one of (those) seven angels
b who had the seven bowls
a' came
c and spoke with me,
d saying,
e "Come, I will show you the judgment on the great prostitute
f who is sitting over many waters.
2a The kings of the earth have practiced promiscuity with her,

c and those dwelling on the earth,
d have become drunk
b' from the wine of her promiscuity."

b) Vision

Move a few steps to stage left.

3a And in (the) spirit he carried me away into a wilderness,
b and I saw a woman *Gesture to imaginary location of Babylon (my suggestion is stage left).*
c sitting on a scarlet beast
d filled with slanderous names, *Tone: "Hint, hint! You've seen this before!"*
e (and it had) seven heads and ten horns.
4a And the woman was clothed in purple
(cloth) and scarlet (cloth),
b and adorned with gold and precious stones and pearls,
c (And she held) a golden cup in her
hand *Amazement at her wealth turns to disgust at next line.*
d that was full of abominations and
the impurities of her promiscuity; *Reading her forehead.*
5a and on her forehead (was) written a name, a mystery:
b "Babylon the great, the mother of prostitutes and
abominations of the earth."
6a And I saw (that) the woman *Surprise.*
b was drunk (on) the blood of the saints,
that is, the blood of the witnesses of Jesus.

c And I was greatly amazed,[18]
d when I saw her.

c) The explanation of the mystery *Indignation.*
17:7a But the angel said to me,
b "Why are you so amazed? *Cranky: Clueless Seer theme.*
c I will tell you the mystery of the woman and the beast
d that bears her,[19]
e that has seven heads and ten horns. *"Hint, hint! You've seen this before!"*

18. Compare with "severely scorched" (16:9a).
19. Compare with 2:3.

8a The beast
b that you saw
a' was,
c but is not,
d but is about to come up from the abyss
e and go away to destruction. Point away.
f And they will be amazed,
g those who dwell on the earth,
h whose the name(s have) not been written (from the foundation of the world)
in the scroll of life.
i (They will be amazed) when they see the beast,
j because it was
k and is not
l and will be present.

Aside:
9a Here is a mind
b that has wisdom:
c the seven heads are seven mountains
d where the woman sits;[20]
e They are also seven kings:
10a five have fallen,
b one is living,
c and the other has not yet come;
d and when he comes,
e he must stay only a little while.
11a And the beast
b that was
c and is not,
a' is both himself[21] an eighth (king),
d and (one) of the seven,
e and it goes to destruction.

20. George B. Caird, *The Revelation of St. John the Divine* (New York: Harper, 1966), 215, suggests "enthroned" (17:1f; cf. 14:6d).
21. Masculine identical pronoun! A clear hint we should expect a person.

12a And the ten horns
b that you saw
c are ten kings
d who have not yet received a kingdom,
e but they are to receive authority as kings for one
hour, together with the beast.
13a These (kings) have one purpose:
b to give their power and authority to the beast.
14a These (kings) will fight against the lamb,
b but the lamb will conquer them,
c because he is Lord of lords and King of kings, *Climaxing.*
d and those with him (are) called and chosen
and faithful." *Pause before new introduction.*

Reduce volume, pace.
15a And (the angel) (said) to me,
b "The waters that you saw,
c where the prostitute is seated,
d are peoples and multitudes and nations and languages.

16a And the ten horns and the beast
b that you saw,
a' these will hate the prostitute
c and will lay her waste[22] and naked,
d and will consume her flesh (pl.),
e and burn her with fire.
17a For God has put it into their hearts
b to do his purpose and to be of one purpose
c (which is) to give their kingdom to the beast
d until the words of God will be fulfilled.

18a And the woman *Slow—this is the punchline!*
b whom you saw
a' is the great city
c that has an (empire) over the kings of the earth."

22. Compare with 18:17a.

2. The destruction of the great city (18:1-24)

Perform beginning as taunt song but with increasing empathy, especially for shipmasters, et al., who scream.

a) A taunt song (vision and audition)

18:1a After these (things) I saw another angel
b coming down from heaven,
c (He had) great authority;
d and the earth was illuminated by his glory.
2a And he shouted with a mighty voice,
b saying,
c "Fallen,
d fallen is Babylon the great!
e It has happened! (Babylon is) a dwelling for demons,
a refuge for every unclean spirit,
a refuge for every unclean bird,
a refuge for every unclean
and hateful beast.

Asyndeton: Intensity, gravity.

Slow for added element—evoke 17:16.

3a For all the nations have drunk the wine of her (passionate promiscuity),
b and the kings of the earth have practiced promiscuity with her,
c and the merchants of the earth have grown rich
from the power of her luxury."

Last element of polysyndeton: expansive: now merchants, too.

b) Summons to flight and revenge (Audition)

4a And I heard another voice from heaven
b saying,
c "Come out (pl.) of her, my people,
d in order that you may not be a partner[23] in her sins,
e and that you may not receive her plagues;
5a for her sins are heaped up as high as[24] heaven.
b Now, God has remembered her injustices.

Pleading

23. Compare with 1:9.
24. Compare with 14:20.

6a Pay her back

Shouting up to heaven.

b in her own coin!
c Repay her double for her works![25]
d And in the cup
e that she has mixed,
d' mix (pl.) her a double.
7a As much as she glorified herself
b and lived luxuriously,
c give (pl.) her that much torment and grief.
d Because in her heart she says,
e 'I am sitting (as) a queen

Falsetto as with Laodicea (3:17).

f and I am no widow,
g and never shall I know grief.'[26]
8a Therefore her plagues will come in a single day
b – death and grief and famine –
c and she will be burned with fire;
d for mighty is the Lord God
e who judges her."

Emphasize "with her" to contrast how they stand at a distance.

c) Three songs of lament
9c And the kings of the earth,
d who (practiced promiscuity) with her
e and lived in luxury (with her),
a they will weep

Gesture: Beat chest as 1:7.

b and beat (their chest) for her[27]
f when they watch the smoke of her burning;
10a while they stand far off because of fear of her torment,

Humor—irony: they stand off while she burns!

b saying,
c "Woe, woe, the great city, Babylon, the mighty city!
d For in a single hour your judgment has come."

25. Caird, *Revelation,* 224.
26. Compare with Laodicea's sayings (3:17).
27. Compare with 1:7e.

11a And the merchants of the earth weep
b and mourn for her,
c since no one buys their cargo anymore,
12a cargo of gold
and of silver
and of precious stones
and of pearls
and of fine linen
and of purple (cloth),
and of silk
and of scarlet (cloth),
and all kinds of scented wood,
and every kind of ivory work,[28]
and all sorts of products made
from costly wood[29]
and ~~of~~ bronze
and ~~of~~ iron
and ~~of~~ marble,
13a and cinnamon
and spice
and incense
such as myrrh
and frankincense
and wine
and olive oil
and fine flour
and wheat
and cattle
and sheep,
and ~~of~~ horses
and ~~of~~ chariots
and ~~of~~ slaves –
(that is) human souls.

Polysyndeton: expansive, slow—"conveys the profound materialism of Rome/Babylon" (Aune, Revelation 17-22, 981).

Punchline.

28. Caird, *Revelation*, 225.

29. David Aune, *Revelation 17-22* (WBC 52C; Nashville, TN: Thomas Nelson, 1998), 981.

Interruption: Address to Babylon

Turn to face imaginary Bablyon off-stage, shouting.

14a And the good life[30] that your soul
desires has gone from you,

Emphasis on soul to connect with slaves above.

b and all the glitter and glamour[31] are lost from you,
c and no one, never, ever will find (it)!"[32]

15a The merchants in these (goods),
b who became rich from her,
a' (they) will stand far off because of fear of her torment,
c while they weep
d and mourn,
16a saying,
b "Woe, woe, the great city,
c clothed in fine linen and in purple (cloth)
and in scarlet (cloth),
d and adorned [with] gold and precious stone and pearl,
17a because in a single hour all this wealth has been
laid waste!"

b And every shipmaster and (seafarer) and sailors and
those who work the sea
c stood far off
18a and screamed[33]

Empathetically.

b when they saw the smoke of her burning,
c saying,
d "What (city was) like the great city?"
19a And they threw dust on their heads
b and screamed,
c weeping
d and mourning,

30. Ibid., 1003.

31. Ibid., 970.

32. G. K. Beale, *The Book of Revelation* (NIGTC; Grand Rapids, MI: 1999), 911.

33. *Krazō* is used elsewhere in Revelation only for the people of God, which suggests greater identification between the shipmasters et al. and the audience.

e saying,
f "Woe, woe, the great city!
g Everyone with a ship at sea
h became rich[34]
g' from her prosperity!
i In a single hour she was laid waste."

Interruption: Address to heaven and audience

Gesture toward heaven, try to recall gesture of 12:12.

20a Rejoice over her, O heaven, and the saints and the apostles
and the prophets!
b For God has judged her for judging you.[35]

d) A symbolic action

21a And a single mighty angel lifted a stone like a
huge millstone
b and hurled (it) into the sea,
c saying,
d "Thus with violence Babylon the great city
will be thrown (down),
e and will not be found any more;[36]

Address to Babylon off-stage

22a and (the) sound of harpists and musicians and flutists
and trumpeters
will not be heard in you any more;
b and artisans of every trade
will not be found in you any more;
c and (the) sound of a millstone
will not be heard in you any more;
23a and (the) light of a lamp
will not shine in you any more;

Both anaphora (p- and phō-) and homoioteleuton (en soi eti) with polysyndeton expanding and emphasizing the deserted city topos; inclusio with 18:2. Slowly building.

34. See Caird, *Revelation*, 225.

35. Aune, *Revelation 17-22*, 1008. Jörns names this a "call to cheer" (*Der Ruf zum Jubel*) with 12:12. K.-P. Jörns, *Das hymnische Evangelium. Untersuchungen zu Aufbau, Funktion und Herkunft der hymnischen*

Stücke in der Johannesoffenbarung (Gütersloh: Mohn, 1971), 140–41. I would add 19:5c-d below, each as a call for God's people to respond.

36. Compare with 12:8.

b and (the) voice of bridegroom and bride
will not be heard in you any more;
c because your merchants were the important people[37]
of the earth,
d because all nations were deceived by your sorcery.
24a And in her was found (the) blood of prophets and saints,
b and all who have been slaughtered
on the earth."

Switch from Babylon focus to audience focus: climax, as prosecutor pointing to accused off-stage

3. In the throne-room again (19:1–10)

a) An audition

Slower, calmer and growing to chorus.

19:1a After these (things) I heard
something like a loud voice from a great multitude
in heaven,
b chanting,
c "Hallelujah!
d (This is) the victory and glory and power of our God,
2a because (God's) judgments (are) true and just!
b because (God) has judged the great prostitute
c who corrupted the earth with her promiscuity,
d and (God) has avenged the blood of his slaves (which
is on her hands)[38]."
3a And a second (time) they chanted,
b "Hallelujah!
c Her smoke goes up into the ages of the ages."
4a And the twenty-four elders and the four living creatures
fell (down)
b and worshiped God,
c the one who is sitting on the throne,
d chanting,
e "Amen. Hallelujah!"

37. Compare with 6:15.
38. See Aune, *Revelation 17-22*, 1015.

5a And a voice came out from the throne
b saying,[39]
c "Praise our God, all (you) his slaves,
d [~~and~~] those who fear (God), small and great."
6a And I heard something like the sound of a
great multitude,
and like the sound of many waters
and like a sound of mighty thunders,

Polysyndeton *and* anaphora: *expanding and increasing in volume. Cf. 14:2.*

b chanting,
c "Hallelujah!
d For the Lord [our] God the Almighty has begun to rule.[40]
7a Let us rejoice
b and exult
c and give God glory,
d because the marriage of the lamb has come,
e and his bride has prepared herself;
8a and she has been given (the right)
b to wear fine linen, bright, pure"—
c for the fine linen (is) the just deeds of the saints.

Asyndeton: *with gravity.*

b) Aside: An angelic revelation

9a And (the angel) said to me,
b "Write (this):
c Blessed are
d those invited to the marriage feast of the lamb."
e Then he said to me,
f "These words from God are true."

---

39. Not chanted; this command to the slaves of God is not itself an expression of worship. Contra Jörns, *Das hymnische Evangelium*, 152, who argues it is a prompt (*Aufforderung*) to praise in hymnic form as Ps 33:2. See note above on 18:20.

40. Compare with 11:17.

Bibliography

Aronoff, Mark, and Janie Rees-Miller, eds. *The Handbook of Linguistics.* Oxford: Wiley-Blackwell, 2003.

Aune, David. *Revelation.* 3 vols. Word Biblical Commentary. Waco, TX: Word, 1997–98.

Bagnall, Roger S. *Everyday Writing in the Græco-Roman East.* Berkeley: University of California Press, 2012.

Barr, David L. *Tales of the End: A Narrative Commentary on the Book of Revelation.* Santa Rosa, CA: Polebridge, 1998.

Bauckham, Richard. *Jesus and the Eyewitnesses: The Gospels as Eyewitness Testimony.* Grand Rapids: Eerdmans, 2006.

____. *Theology of the Book of Revelation.* Cambridge: Cambridge University Press, 1993.

Baynes, Leslie. *The Heavenly Book Motif in Judeo-Christian Apocalypses 200 B.C.E.–200 C.E.* Leiden: Brill, 2011.

Beale, G. K. *The Book of Revelation.* The New International Greek Testament Commentary. Grand Rapids: Eerdmans, 1999.

Betz, Hans Dieter. *Galatians: A Commentary on Paul's Letter to the Churches in Galatia.* Hermeneia. Minneapolis: Fortress Press, 1989.

Blount, Brian K. *Revelation: A Commentary.* The New Testament Library. Louisville: Westminster John Knox, 2009.

Boomershine, Thomas E. "Biblical Megatrends: Towards a Paradigm for the Interpretation of the Bible in Electronic Media." In *SBL Seminar Papers,* 144–57. Atlanta: Scholars Press, 1987.

____. *The Messiah of Peace: A Performance-Criticism Commentary on Mark's Passion-Resurrection Narrative*. Eugene, OR: Cascade, 2015.

____. *Story Journey: An Invitation to the Gospel as Storytelling*. Nashville: Abingdon, 1988.

Botha, Pieter J. J. *Orality and Literacy in Early Christianity*. Eugene, OR: Cascade, 2012.

Byrskog, Samuel. *Story as History—History as Story*. Tübingen: Mohr Siebeck, 2000.

Caird, George. *The Revelation to St. John the Divine*. New York: Harper, 1966.

Callahan, Allan D. "The Language of the Apocalypse." *Harvard Theological Review* 88 (1995): 453–70.

Carlson, Marvin. *Performance: A Critical Introduction*. 2d ed. London: Routledge, 2004.

Carr, David M. *The Formation of the Hebrew Bible: A New Reconstruction*. London: Oxford University Press, 2011.

____. *Writing on the Tablet of the Heart: Origins of Scripture and Literature*. New York: Oxford University Press, 2008.

Charlesworth, James H. and Mordechai Aviam. "Reconstructing First-Century Galilee." In James H. Charlesworth, Brian Rhea, and Petr Pokorny, eds., *Jesus Research: New Methodologies and Perceptions—The Second Princeton-Prague Symposium on Jesus Research, Princeton 2007*, 103–37. Grand Rapids: Eerdmans, 2014.

Conquergood, Dwight. "Performance Studies: Interventions and Radical Research." *The Drama Review* 46, no. 2 (Summer 2002): 145–56.

Culley, Robert C. "Oral Tradition and Biblical Studies." *Oral Tradition* 1, no. 1 (1986): 30-65.

Dewey, Joanna. "From Storytelling to Written Text: The Loss of Early Christian Women's Voices." *Biblical Theology Bulletin* 26, no. 2 (1996): 71–78.

____. "The Survival of Mark's Gospel: A Good Story?" *Journal of Biblical Literature* 123, no. 3 (Fall 2004): 495–507.

____. "Textuality in an Oral Culture: A Survey of the Pauline Traditions." In Joanna Dewey, ed., *Semeia 65: Orality and Textuality in Early Christian Literature*, 37–65. Atlanta: Scholars Press, 1995.

____. "Women on the Way: A Reconstruction of Late First-Century Women's

Storytelling." In Holly E. Hearon and Philip Ruge-Jones, eds., *The Bible in Ancient and Modern Media: Story and Performance*, 36–48. Eugene, OR: Cascade, 2009.

Doan, William, and Terry Giles. *Prophets, Performance, and Power.* London: Continuum, 2005.

Esala, Nathan. "Ideology and Bible Translation: Can Biblical Performance Criticism Help?" *The Bible Translator* 66, no. 3 (2015): 216–29.

Fiensy, David A. "The Galilean Village in the Late Second Temple and Mishnaic Periods." In David A. Fiensy and James Riley Strange, eds., *Galilee in the Late Second Temple and Mishnaic Periods, Volume 1: Life, Culture, and Society*, 177–207. Minneapolis: Fortress Press, 2014.

Foley, John Miles. *Immanent Art: From Structure to Meaning in Traditional Oral Epic.* Indianapolis: Indiana University Press, 1991.

____. *Oral Tradition and the Internet: Pathways of the Mind.* Champaign: University of Illinois Press, 2012.

____. "Words in Tradition, Words in Text: A Response." In Joanna Dewey, ed., *Semeia 65: Orality and Textuality in Early Christian Literature*, 169–80. Atlanta: Scholars Press, 1995.

Fowler, Robert M. "Why Everything We Know about the Bible Is Wrong: Lessons from the Media History of the Bible." In Holly E. Hearon and Philip Ruge-Jones, eds., *The Bible in Ancient and Modern Media: Story and Performance*, 3–18. Eugene, OR: Cascade, 2009.

Friesen, Steven J. *Imperial Cults and the Apocalypse of John.* New York: Oxford University Press, 2001.

____. "Satan's Throne, Imperial Cults and the Social Setting of Revelation." *Journal for the Study of the New Testament* 27, no. 3 (2005): 351–73.

Gerhardsson, Birger. "Mark and the Female Witnesses." In Hermann Behrens, Darlene Loding, and M. T. Roth, ed., *Dumu-E2-Dub-Ba-A: Studies in Honor of Ake W. Sjoberg*, 218–23. Philadelphia: University of Pennsylvania Museum, 1989.

____. *Memory and Manuscript.* Grand Rapids: Eerdmans, 1998 [1961].

Gowan, Donald E. *The Triumph of Faith in Habakkuk.* Atlanta: John Knox, 1976.

Han, Jin H. *Daniel's Spiel: Apocalyptic Literacy in the Book of Daniel.* Lanham, MD: University Press of America, 2008.

Hearon, Holly E. "The Interplay Between Written and Spoken Word in the

Second Testament as Background to the Emergence of Written Gospels." *Oral Tradition* 25, no. 1 (March 2010): 57–74. http://journal.oraltradition.org/issues/25i/hearon.

____. *The Mary Magdalene Tradition: Witness and Counter-Witness in Early Christian Communities.* Collegeville, MN: Michael Glazier, 2004.

Hiebert, Theodore. *God of My Victory: The Ancient Hymn in Habakkuk 3.* Atlanta: Scholars Press, 1986.

Hurtado, Larry W. "Oral Fixation and New Testament Studies?: 'Orality', 'Performance' and Reading Texts in Early Christianity." *New Testament Studies* 60, no. 3 (July 2014): 321–40.

Iverson, Kelly R. "A Centurion's 'Confession': A Performance-Critical Analysis of Mark 15:39." *Journal of Biblical Literature* 130, no. 2 (2011): 329–50.

Johnson, Lee A. "Paul's Epistolary Presence in Corinth: A New Look at Robert W. Funk's Apostolic Parousia." *The Catholic Biblical Quarterly* 68, no. 3 (July 2006): 481–501.

Johnson, William Allen. *Readers and Reading Culture in the High Roman Empire: A Study of Elite Communities.* New York: Oxford University Press, 2010.

____, and Holt N. Parker. *Ancient Literacies: The Culture of Reading in Greece and Rome.* New York: Oxford University Press, 2011.

Jörns, Klaus-Peter. *Das hymnische Evangelium. Untersuchungen zu Aufbau, Funktion und Herkunft der hymnischen Stücke in der Johannesoffenbarung.* Gütersloh: Mohn, 1971.

Keith, Chris. *Jesus against the Scribal Elite: The Origins of the Conflict.* Grand Rapids: Baker Academic, 2014.

____. "Hurtado on Oral Fixation in New Testament Studies." http://historicaljesusresearch.blogspot.com/2014/06/hurtado-on-oral-fixation-in-new.html.

Kelber, Werner. *The Oral and Written Gospel: The Hermeneutics of Speaking and Writing in the Synoptic Tradition, Mark, Paul, and Q.* Philadelphia: Fortress Press, 1983.

____. "Words and Tradition: Words in Time, Words in Space." In Joanna Dewey, ed., *Semeia 65: Orality and Textuality in Early Christian Literature*, 139–67. Atlanta: Scholars Press, 1995.

Kennedy, George. *New Testament Interpretation through Rhetorical Criticism.* Chapel Hill: University of North Carolina Press, 1984.

Kirk, Alan, and Tom Thatcher. *Memory, Tradition, and Text: Uses of the Past in Early Christianity.* Atlanta: SBL Press, 2005.

Klauck, Hans-Josef. *Ancient Letters and the New Testament.* Waco, TX: Baylor University Press, 2006.

Koester, Craig R. *Revelation: A New Translation with Introduction and Commentary.* The Anchor Yale Bible Commentaries. New Haven: Yale University Press, 2014.

Kovacs, Judith L., and Christopher Rowland, with Rebekah Callow. *Revelation: The Apocalypse of Jesus Christ.* Oxford: Blackwell, 2004.

Lee, Margaret E. "My First Experience Performing." http://www.biblicalperformancecriticism.org/index.php/10-news/performance-reflections/101-my-first-experience-performing.

____, and Bernard Brandon Scott. *Sound Mapping the New Testament.* Salem, OR: Polebridge, 2009.

Levine, Lee I. "The Synagogues of Galilee." In David A. Fiensy and James Riley Strange, eds., *Galilee in the Late Second Temple and Mishnaic Periods, Volume 1: Life, Culture, and Society*, 129–50. Minneapolis: Fortress Press, 2014.

Longenecker, Bruce W. *Rhetoric at the Boundaries: The Art and Theology of the New Testament Chain-Link Transition.* Waco, TX: Baylor University Press, 2005.

Lord, Albert B. *The Singer of Tales.* Cambridge: Harvard University Press, 1960.

Loubser, J. A. (Bobby). *Oral and Manuscript Culture in the Bible: Studies on the Media Texture of the New Testament—Explorative Hermeneutics.* Eugene, OR: Cascade, 2013.

Madison, D. Soyini, and Judith Hamera. "Performance Studies at the Intersections." In D. Soyini Madison and Judith Hamera, eds., *The Sage Handbook of Performance Studies*, xi–xxv. Thousand Oaks, CA: Sage, 2006.

Malina, Bruce J. *The New Testament World: Insights from Cultural Anthropology.* 3d ed. Louisville: Westminster John Knox, 2001.

Mathews, Jeanette. *Performing Habakkuk: Faithful Re Enactment in the Midst of Crisis.* Eugene, OR: Wipf & Stock, 2012.

Maxey, James. "Alternative Evaluative Concepts to the Trinity of Bible

Translation." In Piotr Blumczynski and John Gillespie, eds., *Translating Values*, 57-80. New York: Palgrave Macmillan, 2016.

____. *From Orality to Orality: A New Paradigm for Contextual Translation of the Bible*. Eugene, OR: Cascade, 2009.

Maxwell, Kathy. *Hearing Between the Lines: The Audience as Fellow-Worker in Luke-Acts and its Literary Milieu*. London: T&T Clark, 2010.

McLuhan, Marshall. *Understanding Media: The Extensions of Man*. New York: Mentor, 1964.

Metzger, Bruce M. *A Textual Commentary on the Greek New Testament*. 2d ed. Stuttgart: United Bible Societies, 1994.

Mitchell, Margaret M. "New Testament Envoys in the Context of Greco-Roman Diplomatic and Epistolary Conventions: The Example of Timothy and Titus." *Journal of Biblical Literature* 111, no. 4 (Winter 1992): 641–62.

Nässelqvist, Dan. *Public Reading in Early Christianity: Lectors, Manuscripts, and Sound in the Oral Delivery of John 1–4*. Leiden: Brill, 2015.

Niditch, Susan. *Oral World and Written Word*. Louisville: Westminster John Knox, 1996.

Nissinen, Martti. "Spoken, Written, Quoted, and Invented: Orality and Writtenness in Ancient Near Eastern Prophecy." In Ehud Ben Zvi and Michael H. Floyd, eds., *Writings and Speech in Israelite and Ancient Near Eastern Prophecy*, 235–71. Atlanta: SBL Press, 2000.

O'Collins, Gerald, and Daniel Kendall. "Mary Magdalene as Major Witness to Jesus' Resurrection." *Theological Studies* 48 (1987): 631–46.

Oestreich, Bernhard. *Performanzkritik der Paulusbriefe*. Tübingen: Mohr Siebeck, 2012.

Ong, Walter J. *Orality and Literacy: The Technologizing of the Word*. London: Routledge, 1998.

Perry, Peter S. *The Rhetoric of Digressions: Ancient Communication and Rev. 7:1-17 and 10:1—11:13*. Tübingen: Mohr Siebeck, 2009.

____. "'Things Having Lives': Ecology, Allusion, and Performance in Revelation 8:9." *Currents in Theology and Mission* 37, no. 2 (April 2010): 105–13.

Person, Raymond F. *The Deuteronomic History and the Book of Chronicles: Scribal Works in an Oral World*. Atlanta: SBL Press, 2010.

____. "The Role of Memory in the Tradition Represented by the Deuteronomic

History and the Book of Chronicles." Oral Tradition 26, no. 2 (October 2011): 537–50. http://journal.oraltradition.org/issues/26ii/person.

Pippin, Tina. "The Heroine and the Whore." In David Rhoads, ed., *From Every People and Nation: The Book of Revelation in Intercultural Perspective*, 127–45. Minneapolis: Fortress Press, 2005.

Powell, Mark Allan. *What Is Narrative Criticism?* Guides to Biblical Scholarship. Minneapolis: Fortress Press, 1991.

Resseguie, James L. *Narrative Criticism of the New Testament: An Introduction.* Grand Rapids: Baker, 2005.

____. *The Revelation of John: A Narrative Commentary*. Grand Rapids: Baker, 2009.

Rhoads, David. "Performance Criticism: An Emerging Methodology in Second Testament Studies—Part I." *Biblical Theology Bulletin* 36, no. 3 (2006): 118–33.

____. "Performance Criticism: An Emerging Methodology in Second Testament Studies—Part II." *Biblical Theology Bulletin* 36, no. 4 (2006): 164–84.

____. "What Is Performance Criticism?" In Holly E. Hearon and Philip Ruge-Jones, eds., *The Bible in Ancient and Modern Media: Story and Performance*, 83–100. Eugene, OR: Cascade, 2009.

____, Joanna Dewey, and Donald Mitchie. *Mark as Story: An Introduction to the Narrative of a Gospel.* 3d ed. Minneapolis: Fortress Press, 2012.

Ricoeur, Paul. *Hermeneutics and the Human Sciences: Essays on Language, Action and Interpretation.* Edited and translated by J. B. Thompson. London: Cambridge University Press, 1981.

Roberts, Colin H., and T. C. Skeat. *The Birth of the Codex.* New York: Oxford University Press, 1987.

Roberts, J. J. M. *Nahum, Habakkuk, and Zephaniah.* The Old Testament Library. Louisville: Westminster John Knox, 1991.

Rodríguez, Rafael. *Oral Tradition and the New Testament: A Guide for the Perplexed.* London: Bloomsbury/T&T Clark, 2014.

Rossing, Barbara R. *The Choice Between Two Cities: Whore, Bride, and Empire in the Apocalypse*. Harrisburg, PA: Trinity Press International, 1999.

____. *The Rapture Exposed: The Message of Hope in the Book of Revelation*. New York: Basic, 2005.

____. "River of Life in God's New Jerusalem: An Ecological Vision for Earth's Future." *Mission Studies* 16 (January 1999): 136–56.

Royalty, Robert M. *The Streets of Heaven: The Ideology of Wealth in the Apocalypse of John*. Macon, GA: Mercer University Press, 1998.

Ruge-Jones, Philip. "The Word Heard: How Hearing a Text Differs from Reading One." In Holly E. Hearon and Philip Ruge-Jones, eds., *The Bible in Ancient and Modern Media: Story and Performance*, 101–13. Eugene, OR: Cascade, 2009.

Runesson, Anders, Donald D. Binder, and Birger Olsson. *The Ancient Synagogue from Its Origins to 200 C.E.: A Source Book*. Leiden: Brill, 2008.

Runge, Steven E. *Discourse Grammar of the Greek New Testament: A Practical Introduction for Teaching and Exegesis*. Peabody, MA: Hendrickson, 2010.

Sabar, Ariel. "Unearthing the World of Jesus." *Scientific American* 49, no. 6 (January/February 2016): 42–55, 122, 124, 126, 128, 130.

Schechner, Richard. *Performance Studies: An Introduction*. 3d ed. London: Routledge, 2013.

Schüssler-Fiorenza, Elisabeth. *In Memory of Her*. New York: Crossroad, 1983.

Scott, Bernard Brandon. "Blowing in the Wind: A Response." In Joanna Dewey, ed., *Semeia 65: Orality and Textuality in Early Christian Literature*, 181–91. Atlanta: Scholars Press, 1995.

Shiell, William David. *Reading Acts: The Lector and the Early Christian Audience*. Leiden: Brill, 2004.

Shiner, Whitney. *Proclaiming the Gospel: First-Century Performance of Mark*. Harrisburg, PA: Trinity Press International, 2003.

Sperber, Dan, and Deidre Wilson. *Relevance: Communication and Cognition*. 2d ed. Oxford: Wiley-Blackwell, 1996.

Stevens, Gerald L. *Revelation: The Past and Future of John's Apocalypse*. Eugene, OR: Pickwick, 2014.

Swanson, Richard. *Provoking the Gospel: Methods to Embody Biblical Storytelling through Drama*. Cleveland: Pilgrim, 2004.

———. *Provoking the Gospel of Mark: A Storyteller's Commentary Year B*. Cleveland: Pilgrims, 2005.

Thatcher, Tom. *Why John Wrote a Gospel: Jesus—Memory—History*. Louisville: Westminster John Knox, 2005.

Trebilco, Paul R. *Jewish Communities in Asia Minor*. New York: Cambridge University Press, 1991.

Wainwright, Arthur W. *Mysterious Apocalypse: Interpreting the Book of Revelation*. Nashville: Abingdon, 1993.

Ward, Richard, and David Trobisch. *Bringing the Word to Life: Engaging the New Testament through Performing It*. Grand Rapids: Eerdmans, 2013.

Weber, Timothy P. *On the Road to Armageddon: How Evangelicals Became Israel's Best Friend*. Grand Rapids: Baker, 2005.

Wendland, Ernst R. *Orality and the Scriptures: Composition, Translation, and Transmission*. Dallas: SIL, 2013.

____, and J. P. Louw. *Graphic Design and Bible Reading: Exploratory Studies in the Typographical Representation of the Text of Scripture in Translation*. Capetown: Bible Societies of South Africa, 1993.

Westhelle, Vitor. "Between the Colonial and the Postcolonial: A Reading from Brazil." In David Rhoads, ed., *From Every People and Nation: The Book of Revelation in Intercultural Perspective*, 183–99. Minneapolis: Fortress Press, 2005.

Williams, Michael E., and Dennis E. Smith. *The Storyteller's Companion to the Bible: Volume 11, Parables of Jesus*. Nashville: Abingdon, 2006.

Wire, Antoinette Clark. *The Case for Mark Composed in Performance*. Eugene, OR: Cascade, 2011.

Yaghjian, Lucretia B. "Ancient Reading." In Richard Rohrbaugh, ed., *The Social Sciences and New Testament Interpretation*, 206–30. Peabody, MA: Hendrickson, 1996.